STU DE

D0248093

Edexcel A2

Government & Politics

Governing the USA

William Storey

Series Editor: Eric Magee

Philip Allan Updates, an imprint of Hodder Education, an Hachette UK
company, Market Place, Deddington, Oxfordshire OX15 OSE

Orders

Bookpoint Ltd, 130 Milton Park, Abingdon, Oxfordshire OX14 4SB
tel: 01235 827720
fax: 01235 400454
e-mail: uk.orders@bookpoint.co.uk
Lines are open 9.00 a.m.–5.00 p.m., Monday to Saturday, with a 24-hour
message answering service. You can also order through the Philip Allan
Updates website: www.philipallan.co.uk

© Philip Allan Updates 2009

ISBN 978-0-340-98712-4

First printed 2009
Impression number 5 4 3 2 1
Year 2014 2013 2012 2011 2010 2009

This guide has been written specifically to support students preparing for the
Edexcel A2 Government & Politics Unit 4C examination. The content has been
neither approved nor endorsed by Edexcel and remains the sole responsibility
of the author.

Typeset by Phoenix Photosetting, Chatham, Kent
Printed by MPG Books, Bodmin

Hachette UK's policy is to use papers that are natural, renewable and recyclable
products and made from wood grown in sustainable forests. The logging and
manufacturing processes are expected to conform to the environmental
regulations of the country of origin.

P1509

Contents

Introduction

■ ■ ■

Content Guidance

The Constitution

The Supreme Court

Questions and Answers

Introduction

This guide has been written to help you prepare more effectively for the Unit 4C Governing the USA examination for the Edexcel Advanced (A2) GCE in Government & Politics.

Its aim is to provide a clear outline of the way in which the unit is structured and examined, as well as providing you with a summary of the content for each part of the unit. Unit 3C, Representative Processes in the USA, is covered in a separate guide.

The specification at a glance

The unit is divided into four areas, as shown in the table below.

Topic	Content outline
The Constitution	• The principles that underpin the Constitution: how the political system can be organised in ways that protect freedom and promote equality of opportunity
	• The political framework established by the Constitution and the mechanisms included to protect freedom, including federalism
	• Perspectives on how well the Constitution has met the high standards set by the Founding Fathers
The Supreme Court	• Judicial review: how and why the Supreme Court became 'guardian of the Constitution' and the significance of this role
	• Judicial philosophies: viewpoints on how the Supreme Court should use its powers
	• Perspectives on the role played by the Supreme Court in the US political system and the extent of its political power
Congress	• The role that the Founding Fathers *intended* the legislature to play when they designed the political framework
	• The legislative, scrutiny and representative roles of Congress
	• Perspectives on the role *actually* played by Congress in the US political system and the extent to which it matches the Founding Fathers' intentions
The presidency	• The restricted role that the Founding Fathers *intended* the executive branch of government to play when they designed the political framework
	• Formal and informal sources of presidential power in both domestic and foreign policy, and the extent to which they are constrained by the other branches of government
	• Perspectives on the role *actually* played by the executive branch in the US political system, and the extent to which it matches the Founding Fathers' intentions

Freedom and opportunity

There is a theme running through these topics. The Founding Fathers, who wrote the Constitution in 1787 (it came into force in 1789), based the entire political system on the idea that freedom and opportunity could be ensured if political power was limited. The intention was that no one individual (or group) could become powerful enough to take away people's liberties or reserve opportunities for a favoured section of the population at the expense of the remainder.

This guide examines the Founding Fathers' ideas in detail. It then compares them to the ways in which the political institutions that make up the central US government today work in the twenty-first century, assesses whether the relationships between these institutions operate as intended, and provides perspectives (from rival ideological viewpoints) on whether the operation of federal government reflects the goals of the 55 men who designed the system over 200 years ago.

If you can establish a strong understanding of how the three branches of the federal government work, relate them to the constitutional mechanisms intended to regulate their powers (such as federalism, the separation of powers and checks and balances) and fully grasp rival viewpoints on the extent to which these elements combine to live up to the aims of the Founding Fathers, you will do well in this unit.

Skills you need to succeed

The A2 course helps you to build on the skills you developed at AS, while adding new skills that will be invaluable at university and throughout your working career.

Knowledge and understanding

Unit 4C is about the way in which the political system is *supposed* to work. You therefore need to learn about the US Constitution in considerable detail — especially the first three Articles and the Bill of Rights. You also need to learn about the workings of Congress, the Supreme Court and the presidency in similar depth, in order to establish a foundation for assessing whether they *actually* operate as originally intended.

In addition to acquiring this body of knowledge, it is important that you learn and use the vocabulary of US politics, including the words and phrases that are unique to it (e.g. filibuster, pork-barrel). You also need to be able to express yourself clearly, with precision and in concise terms, by mastering the political language encountered at both AS and A2.

Application

At this academic level, there will rarely be a time when it is appropriate for you to provide all the information you have. In response to all A2 political questions, you will be expected to apply your knowledge and understanding selectively, according to the issues you are being asked to address.

Analytical skills

You will be expected to explain a point of view effectively, even if you do not agree with it. Being able to understand all political perspectives and explain them, regardless of your personal opinions, is one of the most important skills you have to demonstrate in exams, and is worthy of the highest marks.

Evaluation

You have to demonstrate the ability to weigh up the merits of competing viewpoints. Evaluation means much more than comparing the number of points that are made on two sides of an argument and deciding in favour of the side with the longer list. It means applying mature judgement to the quality and weight of those arguments. One opinion may be supported by a dozen valid points, all of which are weak or insubstantial. A rival opinion may be supported by just a few points that are stronger or more substantial.

Synoptic skills

All the skills outlined above will help you to understand information and arguments, and to promote well informed, thoughtful discussion. Such intense focus, however, can cause people to lose sight of the bigger picture.

In the final analysis, the study of US politics is about what the system is intended to achieve and whether it does so. Your ability to acquire knowledge, identify the most relevant aspects of that knowledge, analyse viewpoints on specific aspects of the political system and weigh up the strengths and weaknesses of those viewpoints is what will help you to reach and express useful conclusions about the US political system and its processes.

The A-level course, therefore, also promotes skills that ensure you keep the whole political system in mind when concentrating on any single aspect of that system. This is known as the development of synoptic skills. For each aspect of the course that you are studying, you will be expected to demonstrate that you can do the following:

- **Identify viewpoints or perspectives.** In the case of US political institutions, this means establishing and evaluating the extent to which each of the institutions are roughly equal in power (i.e. whether there is a *balance* between them) and the extent to which they are able to act as a constraint on any other branch that appears to be expanding its powers (i.e. the extent to which they effectively *check* each other). For each institution, there are rival views on the role they play in the overall system. For example, is the Supreme Court too powerful, effectively making laws while not being held accountable? Or is it playing the essential constitutional role of protecting minorities from a 'tyranny of the majority'?
- **Recognise the nature and extent of the rivalry between these viewpoints.** Continuing the example of the Supreme Court, the existence of rival views on its role is a source of deep division in US society, leading to pressure groups being prepared to spend millions of dollars in support of nominees to the Supreme Court

or against candidates they oppose. In this context, you will need to explain the significance of appointments to the Supreme Court: why some Americans believe that democracy itself may be threatened if the wrong choice is made, while others believe that the Bill of Rights will become meaningless unless the right judges are appointed.

How to develop these skills

There is a range of learning strategies that will help you to do well at A-level.

Classroom learning

Because of the way in which each part of the course has an impact on every other part, consistent lesson attendance is vital. With all the demands of the final year at school or college (university open days, interviews, leadership responsibilities, course-work requirements in other subjects etc.) or of fitting in a course around work and family, it can be all too easy to miss a few lessons. However, you should be aware that even a limited number of absences will have an impact on your overall under-standing.

Textbook learning

Given the depth of understanding required to achieve the highest grades at A-level, the work done in the classroom needs to be reinforced by reading a textbook. As a topic is being covered by your teacher, you should read the relevant sections of the textbook between lessons and, ideally, read it again as a whole once the topic has been completed.

This not only reinforces your understanding of the issues but also helps you to build the political vocabulary that you need in order to properly understand exam questions and to provide the kind of concise responses that are essential under the time pressure of exams. The structured approach of textbooks will also help you to develop the academic writing style used in the best essays.

Wider reading, listening and viewing

You are expected to have a sufficient level of awareness of current affairs to be able to discuss political issues in the light of any recent developments and to illustrate your points with relevant up-to-date examples.

UK newspapers

You can keep reasonably up to date by regularly reading the international section of UK newspapers such as *The Times*, the *Guardian*, the *Telegraph*, the *Independent* and the *Financial Times*. The *Guardian* website also offers substantial background infor-mation on US politics.

Magazines

The US section of *The Economist* is an excellent resource for US politics. The final article in this section, 'Lexington', always offers a viewpoint on an aspect of US politics that helps to develop the analytical, evaluative and synoptic skills outlined above.

In comparison, the international versions of the two best-known US current affairs magazines, *Time* and *Newsweek*, can be quite limited in their coverage of US politics.

US newspapers

The two prestigious 'newspapers of record' in the USA, the *New York Times* and the *Washington Post*, have online editions. If you subscribe (which you can do free of charge), the headlines will be sent to you by e-mail each day. You can scroll down, see which stories look promising, and click on those you wish to read. You can then either retain or delete the e-mail. This is an excellent way of keeping up to date.

Television and radio

The programmes that should have become a standard feature of life while you were studying AS politics, *Channel 4 News*, BBC2's *Newsnight* and BBC Radio 4's *Today Programme* and *PM,* are also valuable resources for US politics at A2. Additionally, anyone with access to the internet would benefit from tuning in to NPR (National Public Radio, the US equivalent of the BBC), which manages to combine thoughtful, in-depth news coverage with a calming, relaxed atmosphere. Some digital television stations also screen late-night talk shows from the USA that provide light-hearted but informative commentary on the latest political developments, for example *The Daily Show* on More4.

US political websites

All the main US news organisations have websites that provide political coverage and background materials. There are also sites dedicated entirely to politics, such as *Real Clear Politics*, which brings together news articles and commentaries from (mainly right-wing) newspapers across the USA; sites dedicated to an aspect of US politics, such as *270towin*, which focuses on presidential elections; and blogs, such as the *Daily Kos*, which provides a forum for left-wing political activists. Most textbooks guide students towards the best websites for each topic as it is studied.

Testing these skills in exams

The knowledge and academic skills of students are tested in written examinations. There is no coursework.

The Unit 4C examination can be taken in either January or June.

It will always include questions on all four topics:
- the Constitution
- the judiciary (the Supreme Court)
- the legislature (Congress)
- the executive (the presidency)

The exam lasts for 1 hour 30 minutes. In that time, you will have to respond to two types of question: short-answer questions and essay questions.

Short-answer questions

There will be five of these questions in Section A of the exam and you will have to choose *three* of them to answer. Each response is worth 15 marks and should take about 15 minutes to complete.

Knowledge and understanding

In each of the short-answer questions, the examiner will be considering the quality of your knowledge and understanding of the key feature of US politics that is at the heart of the question. So, for example, in your answer to the question 'How flexible is the Constitution of the USA?', you would be expected to demonstrate an awareness of the formal mechanisms for amending the Constitution (i.e. knowledge) but also to show that there are informal ways of doing so through Supreme Court interpretation (i.e. understanding).

Analysis and evaluation

The examiner will also be considering the quality of your analysis and evaluation. Thus, in the case of the question on the flexibility of the Constitution, you would be expected to demonstrate the ability to explain (analyse) competing views among Americans as to whether the mechanisms for amending the Constitution make it too flexible or not flexible enough, or whether the Founding Fathers struck the right balance between entrenching rights and the need to keep the Constitution up to date.

You would also be expected to demonstrate the ability to weigh up (evaluate) the significance of points being made. For example, it is questionable whether the Constitution would have been flexible enough to remain largely unchanged over two centuries if it were not for the informal methods of updating it. Your answer would therefore be expected to convey an understanding of the significance of the role of the Supreme Court. If it appears to the examiner that you are simply listing points memorised in advance but not applying maturity of judgement to them (e.g. your conclusion is that three points outweigh two simply because there are more of them), you will not be awarded many marks for the quality of your analysis and evaluation.

Linking

Examiners expect you to be able to link these skills together, demonstrating an ability to construct and communicate coherent arguments, making use of a range of appropriate vocabulary and examples in one articulate response. If you produce a three-paragraph answer, with one paragraph providing evidence of knowledge and understanding, one providing evidence of analysis and another providing evidence of evaluation, the examiner is not likely to be impressed. The best responses to short-answer questions use analytical and evaluative skills to build seamlessly to a conclusion.

Examples of how this is done well, and not so well, are found in the Question and Answer section of this guide.

Essay questions

There will be three essay questions in Section B of the exam and you have to choose *one* of them to answer. This is worth 45 marks and should take about 45 minutes to complete.

Developing an argument

Although examiners will be looking for the skills outlined above, far more is required in an essay than in a short-answer question. In the additional time available, you are expected to develop an argument in response to the question. This means:

- **deciding** your answer to the question
- **persuading** the reader of the merits of your case by presenting the arguments that support your conclusion
- **explaining** why the position you are defending is contested, by outlining the counter-argument (which will inevitably include acknowledging the weaknesses in the argument you have made)
- **defending** your position by arguing that the counter-arguments are outweighed by the case you are making, even when the weaknesses of your viewpoint are taken into account

In this exercise, you are doing more than putting forward two points of view ('some say this, while others say that') and evaluating the strengths of the two arguments in your conclusion. You are developing a case that one set of arguments (note: these are academic arguments, not personal opinions) is stronger than a rival set of arguments and, in doing so, evaluating points of view throughout your essay.

Synoptic skills

Done successfully, the above involves evidence of synoptic skills, which are defined as 'the ability to identify differing viewpoints or perspectives' and 'an awareness of how these viewpoints affect the interpretation of political events or issues and shape the conclusions drawn'.

Examples of how this is done well, and not so well, are found in the Question and Answer section of this guide.

How this guide will help you

This guide is not a substitute for a textbook. There is a lot to learn in preparation for the exam and in-depth reading is essential if you are to perform at the highest levels.

However, especially as part of your revision, this guide will help you make effective use of all the knowledge, understanding and skills you have developed. In particular, it will provide you with:

- reassurance that you have understood the entire specification
- confidence that you have fully explored the main themes that are likely to be the focus of exam questions

- useful examples that demonstrate how the skills you have developed throughout the course can be successfully combined with your knowledge and understanding

All the issues that you are expected to know about, and be able to analyse, are covered in the Content Guidance section.

Sample questions and answers, together with examiner comments, are provided in the Question and Answer section at the end of this guide.

Content
Guidance

This section provides you with a concise overview of the knowledge needed for this unit. The topics covered are:
- The Constitution
- The Supreme Court
- Congress
- The presidency

It outlines how the US political system operates and examines rival points of view on how well the system works. In many cases there are just two viewpoints, criticising or defending aspects of the political processes covered in the unit, but in some cases there is a range of opinions — or there are groups that share the same objective but for different reasons.

Above all, this section sets these debates in the wider context of the overall aims of the Founding Fathers when they designed the political framework of the USA, to promote freedom and equality of opportunity by keeping politicians in check. Accordingly, it provides you with the means to develop an effective argument in response to questions requiring you to reach a reasoned conclusion about the extent to which each aspect of the US political system contributes towards, or hinders, fulfilment of the Founding Fathers' objectives.

The Constitution

Background to the US Constitution

The Constitution of the USA was designed by 55 men, now known as the Founding Fathers. They came together at a convention, held in Philadelphia in 1787, to review the system of government that had been set up after the Declaration of Independence around 10 years earlier in 1776.

This system, known as the Articles of Confederation, had been based on the central idea of the Declaration of Independence: that the UK monarch had failed to respect the liberties that all people were entitled to because of the unrestricted nature of the power enjoyed by him. The abuse of power was seen as the result of the political system in the UK, rather than because of the personality of the king. The Articles of Confederation were therefore designed to severely limit the powers of the national government precisely so that no monarch-like figure could emerge and threaten the liberties of the people. In short, having fought a war of independence, Americans were determined to ensure that there would never be a US equivalent of the British monarch.

However, their system had created a central government so weak that it proved unable to fulfil even its most basic obligation of binding the country, as rivalry and disputes erupted between the 13 original states — hence the need for the Philadelphia Constitutional Convention.

Challenges of producing a Constitution

The Founding Fathers had two main issues to address:
- creating a political system for themselves and future generations that remained faithful to the central idea of the Declaration of Independence (i.e. ensuring that the political system could not be used by any individual or group to build excessive power and use that power to infringe liberty), while at the same time ensuring that government had enough power to run the country effectively
- satisfying concerns that a more powerful central government might become an instrument of the states with the largest populations, allowing them to impose their will on the states with smaller populations

This second challenge brought to the fore a particularly thorny issue: slavery. By 1787, many of the states with larger populations (mainly in the north) were moving towards the abolition of slavery. Southern states, dependent on slavery for their prosperity, feared that a strong central government might be used by the North to force them to give up the practice. They were determined to defend their interests and, to a large extent, they were successful. The slave trade was allowed to continue until at least

1808, a further 21 years after the convention; slaves who escaped to a free state would have to be returned and, when calculating the number of state representatives for the legislature, states would be allowed to include slaves in the count, with five slaves being considered the equivalent of three free people (the 'three-fifths rule'). The only concessions that the North was able to extract from the slave-holding states were an acceptance that the slave trade would not be allowed to continue indefinitely and that the three-fifths rule would apply not only to representation in Congress but also to the level of taxes that states would have to contribute to the central government (contrary to the South's initial demand that slaves be counted only for the purposes of representation and not for taxes).

The significance of this arrangement is considered on page 28, under 'Challenging the Constitution'.

With the issue of slavery addressed, the convention focused on the first challenge: providing the central government with adequate powers, while ensuring that those powers could not be used to infringe liberties.

Federalists v anti-federalists

- The Founding Fathers who believed that the highest priority was providing the central government with adequate powers became known as **federalists**.
- The Founding Fathers who believed that the highest priority was protecting people from central government power became known as **anti-federalists**.

Both agreed that the central government needed more power and that there had to be safeguards against the misuse of this power. The difference was that the federalists advocated a significant increase in power, with limited safeguards, while the anti-federalists wanted any increases in power to be kept to a minimum, with stringent safeguards.

On balance, during the convention the federalists achieved more of their aims than their opponents. However, during the process of the states deciding whether to accept the document drafted by the convention (ratification), some of the anti-federalists' aims were achieved.

Powers of the federal government

Under the Constitution, the central government (referred to from this point as the federal government) was much stronger than it had been under the Articles of Confederation, when it had consisted of just a legislature, with weak powers and no executive or judiciary.

The federal government consists of Congress, the presidency and the Supreme Court.

Congress

Article 1 of the Constitution covers the legislature. Putting it first reflected the intention of the Founding Fathers that the legislature — not the executive — would be the main policy-making body of the government. Consequently, Article 1 goes into great detail about what powers Congress should have and what powers it would not have. This is set out in section 8 of Article 1.

Congress was specifically prohibited from passing certain types of law, such as *ex post facto* laws that punish a person for an action that was legal at the time the act took place. On the other hand, the Constitution controversially included the 'elastic clause', providing Congress with the power to pass any 'necessary and proper' law to fulfil its roles.

Congress is dealt with in more detail later in this guide (see pages 38–51).

The presidency

Article 2 of the Constitution covers the executive. Although the Founding Fathers intended the legislature to take responsibility for initiating policy, the Constitution provides for the president to make an annual 'State of the Union Address', in which he can 'recommend...such measures as he shall judge necessary'. However, most of Article 2 is devoted to powers to be used by the president in order to *implement* the laws that Congress was expected to devise and pass. These include appointing ambassadors and being commander-in-chief of the armed forces (for foreign policy), as well as appointing the heads of government departments (for putting laws into effect).

Where the Constitution gives the executive branch specific responsibility for taking the initiative, such as the negotiation of treaties and choosing federal judges, Senate approval is required.

Considering the Founding Fathers' overriding concern to prevent the emergence of a monarch-like figure, the Constitution is surprisingly vague on the president's powers, and covers them in far less detail than is the case with the Article on Congress. Whether, despite this, the presidency has played the role intended for it by the Founding Fathers is the main focus of a separate topic in this guide (see pages 51–58).

The Supreme Court

Article 3 of the Constitution covers the judiciary. It is even vaguer than the Article on the presidency, specifying only that a Supreme Court was to be established and the types of cases it would hear. Notably, it did not address the question of how the Constitution should be interpreted when the need should arise. As the Constitution is a legal document (it sets out the rules for the political system), it would seem logical that judges would be responsible for explaining how it should be applied to particular situations, i.e. judicial review.

The significance of this omission, and the subsequent decision by the Supreme Court that it would take responsibility for interpreting the Constitution, is the main focus of a separate topic in this guide, examining whether the judiciary has played the role intended for it by the Founding Fathers (see pages 29–38).

Safeguards on federal government power

Unquestionably, the Constitution increased the power of the federal government compared to its powers under the Articles of Confederation. To limit the likely danger to freedom arising from this situation, the Constitution adopted a series of strategies:

- **Federalism.** The Founding Fathers aimed to limit the ability of the federal government *as a whole* from increasing its powers. They wanted to ensure that the individual states would take responsibility for *all* policy areas apart from those clearly awarded to the federal government. This is known as federalism. The intended result of federalism was that the vast majority of political decisions would be made by people from local communities, known to their local communities and accountable to their local communities. (Separately, the Founding Fathers addressed the relationships and interaction between the states in Article 4 of the Constitution.)
- **Separation of powers.** The Founding Fathers aimed to keep the different branches of the federal government separate, thereby limiting their ability to work together to expand their powers (which, if it happened, would undermine federalism). This is known as separation of powers.
- **Bicameralism.** Reflecting the Founding Fathers' expectation that Congress would be the most powerful branch of government, an additional form of separation was introduced into the legislature. Congress was made bicameral, consisting of two chambers (or houses), the House of Representatives and the Senate, which would work together in some respects (for example law making) but which would also have distinct responsibilities and powers in other respects (for example the impeachment of people holding high office in the other two branches).
- **Checks and balances.** To reinforce separation of powers, each branch of government was given responsibility for ensuring that the others used their powers appropriately and, especially, acting as a check on any attempts by another branch to exceed its powers. (For these checks to work effectively, the powers of each branch need to be roughly in proportion to each other or, put another way, in balance with each other. If not, one branch may be able to exceed its powers and the others may not be able to do anything about it.) These checks, by their very nature, tended to introduce competition and rivalry between the branches and reduce the likelihood of them cooperating to undermine the limitations on their political power.
- The Founding Fathers were concerned that circumstances could arise that would lead to one section of society (they called political allies 'factions'; today they are

called political parties) gaining dominance of both elected branches of government (Congress and the presidency) and then use their political power to appoint supporters to the third, unelected, branch (the Supreme Court). If this happened, the four safeguards outlined above could become effectively meaningless. The Founding Fathers put in place a variety of measures to avert this outcome:

- **Staggered terms of office**: members of the House of Representatives serve for 2 years; the president serves for 4 years; Senators serve for 6 years. Thus, even if one party wins all three elections in a year when they all coincide (as happened in 2004, when the Republican Party was victorious, and in 2008, when the Democrats won all three contests), the party has to be mindful that within 2 years the members of the House of Representatives will face another election and the voters will have an opportunity to punish any perceived abuse of power by the party.
- **Indirect elections**: the Founding Fathers, who treated democracy with suspicion for fear that it could lead to 'mob rule', gave the voters a direct say in only one election. Senators were chosen by state legislatures (until a constitutional amendment in 1913) and the president is chosen by an **Electoral College** which, in part, was designed to ensure that if the 'mob' made an irrational choice then the electors could overrule them.
- **Fixed election dates**: the Founding Fathers' lack of faith in ordinary voters led them to fear that the electorate could be manipulated by skilful politicians if those politicians had the discretion to choose the date of elections. They believed that those in power would either capitalise on situations that boosted their popularity to call an election and win another term in office or, more ominously, engineer a crisis that would make the voters wary of a change of leadership or justify postponing an election. Consequently, federal elections are *always* held on the first Tuesday of November of even-numbered years (provided the first Tuesday does not fall on 1 November), even during a major national crisis such as a war, as happened in 1944.
- **Constitutional amendment.** Finally, the Founding Fathers wanted to ensure that politicians, frustrated by all these constraints, would find it difficult to change the Constitution in ways that increased their powers (even if with the genuine conviction that, with more power, they could better serve the people). Consequently, the Founding Fathers put in place a series of challenging hurdles for amending the Constitution (see below). These were intended to ensure that the Constitution would be changed only if there was overwhelming agreement that the political system was in need of improvement.

These safeguards were not sufficient for the anti-federalists. Among the additional measures they proposed was the **recall** of politicians accused of poor performance or misuse of power (a procedure that had been included in the Articles of Confederation and is found in many state constitutions). Most importantly, for the anti-federalists, was the inclusion of a Bill of Rights; when the convention ended, they campaigned hard in the states to have the Constitution rejected unless a Bill of Rights was included.

Amending the Constitution

There are two ways in which the Constitution of the USA can be amended, but only the first method has been used:

- A proposed amendment is introduced to Congress; both houses of Congress support the amendment by a two-thirds majority; three quarters of the state legislatures (currently 38) vote to support (ratify) the amendment; it becomes a part of the Constitution.
- Three quarters of the states pass a resolution calling for a convention that can then amend the Constitution in the same way as the Philadelphia Convention of 1787.

Summary of the Constitution

Branch of government	Powers	Limitations
Congress (House of Representatives and Senate)	• To pass federal laws • To scrutinise the work of the executive branch • To alter the number of judges in the Supreme Court and to set up other federal courts • To represent the interests of the voters	• Federalism — intended to limit the powers exercised by the government • Bicameralism — with each chamber responsible for checking the other • Certain types of law specifically prohibited by the Constitution, such as *ex post facto* laws • Legislation can be vetoed by the president • Fixed election dates and staggered elections to limit the ability to work with other politicians elected to federal positions to expand their powers
The presidency	• To make the State of the Union Address — providing an opportunity to make policy proposals • To veto federal legislation • To make appointments to executive departments and courts • To negotiate and agree treaties • To act as commander-in-chief of the armed forces	• Federalism — intended to limit the powers exercised by the government • Legislation, if vetoed by the president, can still become law with a vote of two thirds of both houses of Congress • All appointments must be confirmed by a majority vote in the Senate • All treaties must be ratified by a two-thirds vote in the Senate

		• While the president can order armed forces into action, only Congress is permitted to formally declare war • Fixed election dates and staggered elections to limit the ability to work with other politicians elected to federal positions to expand their powers
The Supreme Court	• The cases that may come before the court are defined • Jury trials are guaranteed • Specific rules on treason trials are set out	• Choice of judges determined by the president, confirmed by the Senate

Ratification of the Constitution

The final Article of the Constitution specified that each state form a special convention to decide whether or not to accept the document drawn up by the Founding Fathers. This meant that ordinary people, not just established leaders, had a say in the process and that a lively debate accompanied the ratification process. It became clear from this debate that the Constitution would not be accepted in a number of states unless a Bill of Rights was added. The process lasted until May 1790, when Rhode Island became the last state to approve the Constitution. It formally came into effect when, in accordance with Article 7, the ninth state — New Hampshire — ratified it on 21 June 1788.

The Bill of Rights

The drafting and adoption of the Bill of Rights was the first task of Congress. The Bill of Rights makes up the first ten amendments to the Constitution and was adopted in 1791. The rights it protects are as follows:

Amendment	Rights protected
First Amendment	Freedom of religion; freedom of speech; freedom of the press; freedom of assembly (the right to demonstrate)
Second Amendment	Freedom to own firearms (although this may be regulated by Congress and state governments)
Third Amendment	Government is prohibited from forcing homeowners to provide lodgings for soldiers (no longer relevant in the modern USA)
Fourth Amendment	The police are prohibited from searching a person, or home, or possessions without being able to demonstrate that they have good cause (in practice this means a search warrant signed by a judge)

Fifth Amendment	People who have been arrested are entitled not to testify against themselves (the right to remain silent); the authorities must demonstrate that they have sufficient evidence to justify a trial; a person cannot be tried for a criminal offence if he or she has already been acquitted (the 'double jeopardy' rule); the government can only take property for public use (e.g. to build a dam) if fair compensation is paid
Sixth Amendment	Anyone who is to be tried for an alleged offence must have as speedy a trial as possible; the accused is entitled to know all the charges and to hear all the evidence against him or her; the accused is entitled to prepare a defence; the accused is entitled to a jury trial
Seventh Amendment	People involved in civil disputes (such as property disputes between neighbours) are entitled to a jury trial unless both parties agree not to
Eighth Amendment	Judges are prohibited from imposing unreasonable bail conditions on a suspect; sentences for people convicted of a crime must be proportionate to the crime
Ninth Amendment	Rights are not limited to those specified in the Bill of Rights (any rights not mentioned are covered by this amendment)
Tenth Amendment	Any powers not specifically given to the federal government belong to the states (this amendment reinforces the federalism principle in the Constitution)

Subsequent amendments to the Constitution

Since the adoption of the Bill of Rights in 1791, only a further 17 amendments have been added. These can be roughly divided into four categories:

- amendments that overturn Supreme Court decisions, such as the Eleventh and Sixteenth amendments
- the 'civil rights' amendments (Thirteenth, Fourteenth and Fifteenth), which abolished slavery and, in principle, entitled African-Americans to take their place as full citizens of the USA; the Twenty-Fourth Amendment, which abolished a practice that was used to deny African-Americans the vote, could be added to this category
- amendments that affect the way that government works, such as the Twenty-Second Amendment, which limits presidents to two terms in office, or that extend the right to vote; the majority of amendments fall into this category, including those that gave the vote to women (the Nineteenth Amendment), lowered the voting age to 18 (the Twenty-Sixth Amendment) and gave the residents of the District of Columbia the right to vote in presidential elections (the Twenty-Third Amendment)

- the two Prohibition amendments: the Eighteenth Amendment, which prohibited the sale of alcoholic drinks, and the Twenty-First Amendment, which reversed Prohibition, 14 years later

Federalism

Dual federalism

When the Constitution was written, it was widely understood that the federal government and the states would exercise different, separate powers. The federal government would be responsible for all foreign affairs, national defence and all interstate matters (such as trade that crossed state boundaries); the states would be responsible for everything else, including any powers not specifically mentioned in the Constitution (known as 'reserved powers'). For most Americans, this meant that the majority of decisions affecting them would be made by their state government which, in principle, best understood them and had their interests at heart. This relationship between the states and the federal government is known as 'dual federalism'.

In practice, the balance between the two tiers of government was never as neat as dual federalism suggests. During the First World War, for example, the government took direct control of industries that were essential to the war effort and states did not always look after the best interests of *all* their citizens, for example in the South where African Americans looked to the federal courts to protect their interests *from* state governments that practised racial segregation.

Cooperative federalism

When the Great Depression struck, in the 1930s, the balance between the states and the federal government was decisively altered. The states did not have the resources to help citizens who had lost their jobs and, often, their homes. The federal government did have the resources and it used them, in the New Deal, to help those who were suffering and to stimulate the economy. However, this meant federal government involvement in welfare matters that had previously been considered the exclusive responsibility of the states. This changed, overlapping relationship between the states and federal government is known as 'cooperative federalism'.

Notwithstanding the clear need to help those who were in no position to help themselves, the New Deal was fiercely resisted by conservatives in the 1930s as undermining the principle of federalism and weakening the most important constitutional protection of liberty. Even in the twenty-first century, some conservatives regard the New Deal as the start of a slippery slope leading to ever-greater government and, consequently, reduced freedom. Liberals, in contrast, greatly admire the way in which the Constitution allowed the federal government to step in at a time of crisis and make productive use of people who would otherwise have been idle as a result of mass unemployment.

Cooperative federalism continued after the Great Depression had ended, as the federal government continued to play a major role through the Second World War and the Cold War.

Creative federalism

In the 1960s, the relationship between the states and federal government changed again. President Lyndon Johnson launched his Great Society programme, designed to end poverty in the USA. In his view, the states had never made a serious effort to tackle the concentrated pockets of poverty, often in the cities (such as Los Angeles' South Central district), and could not be relied on to do so. Therefore, his programme often bypassed state governments and worked directly with city or local authorities to implement anti-poverty projects. This further advance of the federal government into matters traditionally seen as the responsibility of the states is known as 'creative federalism'.

The Great Society programme provoked a backlash, however. Americans of almost all political persuasions agreed that federalism was in danger of becoming meaningless, as policies concerning communities up to 3,000 miles (4,800 km) away were being made in Washington DC.

New federalism

Since President Johnson left office in 1969, almost every president, both Republican and Democrat, has introduced programmes to re-empower the states and restore a balance closer to the original model of dual federalism. These programmes, although they vary quite significantly, are collectively known as 'new federalism'. In brief, they have worked as follows:

- **President Nixon (Republican, 1969–74).** Nixon's programme, called General Revenue Sharing, allowed the states to spend a greater proportion of their federal grants as they chose.
- **President Carter (Democrat, 1977–81).** Carter continued the General Revenue Sharing programme of his predecessor, but also cut the amount of federal grants available to the states so that they would have to become more self-dependent.
- **President Reagan (Republican, 1981–89).** Reagan made sharp cuts to funds available to the states, especially for welfare payments, as soon as he took office. He offered the states a new arrangement, reminiscent of dual federalism (called 'swaps'), in which they would take full responsibility for some welfare programmes while the federal government would take over others in their entirety. The increased cost to the states of such an arrangement led them to reject the proposal.
- **President Clinton (Democrat, 1993–2001).** Clinton oversaw an economic boom that led to the states building up surplus funds, in many cases for the first time since the 1920s. These funds were then used to pioneer new policy ideas that suited the states' needs and priorities, for example Wisconsin started a programme to extend school choice by issuing families with education vouchers that could be used in any school, whether state-run or private.

- **President George W. Bush (Republican, 2001–09).** Although committed to new federalism in principle, President George W. Bush responded to the attacks of 11 September 2001 by increasing government control over any policy that related to national security. Then, when the economy deteriorated sharply in 2008, he introduced an economic stimulus plan that included substantial payments to struggling state governments.
- **President Obama (Democrat, 2009–).** The first action of President Obama, taking office in the midst of an economic crisis, was an economic stimulus plan on an even greater scale than that of his predecessor.

Overall, new federalism has illustrated the difficulty of achieving a relationship between the states and the federal government that resembles the balance expected by the Founding Fathers.

The reason that federalism has taken so many forms is that none has worked effectively. The only time that the states have enjoyed a resurgence has been during an economic boom. Whenever there has been a national crisis, the federal government has either chosen to assert dominance over the states or has been required to do so, often with the full backing of states that have been powerless to cope with events.

Assessment of the Constitution

As it has not been substantially revised since it was introduced well over 200 years ago, the Constitution appears to have served the American people well through all the changes that have happened during that time.

However, many Americans are critical of aspects of the Constitution and would like to see it reformed. The nature of these criticisms and the preferred reforms vary across the US political spectrum.

Conservatives and the Constitution

In many ways, modern conservatives share the objections made by anti-federalists when the Constitution was created. Both groups share the view that a powerful federal government is incompatible with liberty and that the growth of government over the past two centuries has eroded liberty. They have been especially alarmed at the way in which the federal government has come to share, or take over, responsibilities that once belonged exclusively to the states (see above, under 'Federalism').

In addition, conservatives disapprove of how, since the 1960s, the Supreme Court has interpreted the Fourth, Fifth, Sixth and Eighth amendments to strengthen the rights of suspects and convicted criminals. In their view, this has weakened the law-enforcement authorities and hence also the protection offered to law-abiding citizens.

As ardent supporters of new federalism (a policy that also attracts support from non-conservatives), conservatives would like to see the Constitution amended in ways that more effectively limit the size and scope of the federal government:

- They would like to see a 'balanced-budget amendment' passed, which would prohibit the federal government from operating at a deficit. This would have the effect of forcing the government either to raise taxes to fund its programmes (especially welfare programmes) or to leave responsibility for welfare to the states.
- They would also like to see appointed to the Supreme Court judges who will reinterpret the Bill of Rights in ways that protect the law-abiding citizens and not the law breakers.
- One conservative faction — social conservatives, who would like to see the political system used to promote moral behaviour — favours additional constitutional amendments that would prohibit abortion and same-sex marriage.

Campaigns led by conservatives to change the Constitution have enjoyed limited success. Between 1975 and 1991, a proposal to set up a constitutional convention (the method of amending the Constitution that has not yet been used) in order to pass a balanced-budget amendment won the support of 32 state legislatures — just one state short of the number needed for the convention to take place. In 2006, a proposed amendment to make same-sex marriage unconstitutional received a majority of the votes in the House of Representatives, although it did not meet the two-thirds majority needed in both houses of Congress.

On the other hand, there are some aspects of the Constitution that enjoy strong support among conservatives:

- Conservatives are fierce defenders of the Second Amendment, which they see as providing people with the final resort of defending themselves if the government should ever become tyrannical.
- Although many Americans find it frustrating when the elected branches are controlled by different parties and fail to cooperate with each other, conservatives often welcome this situation. It serves to limit federal government activity, of which, in their view, there is too much.
- In recent years there have been some signs of the Supreme Court tending to interpret the Constitution in ways that meet with the approval of conservatives.

Liberals and the Constitution

Just as modern conservatives share the concerns of the anti-federalists among the Founding Fathers, modern liberals can be seen as the heirs to the federalists of the 1780s. In common with this faction, liberals place great emphasis on the beneficial role of government. Whereas anti-federalists and contemporary conservatives see government power leading directly to a loss of freedom, associating increased government power with decreasing liberty, liberals have welcomed government intervention that has improved people's quality of life (especially the poor and vulnerable in society). At times, therefore, the greatest concern for liberals has been not the growth of government power but rather the constitutional restrictions on the government's ability to do more to help those in need of support.

For example, during the first term of President F. D. Roosevelt, implementation of the New Deal programmes was hampered by the Supreme Court upholding challenges by conservatives that federalism was being undermined, and the Great Society programme would have had a greater chance of success if it had not been seen as contrary to the spirit of the Constitution.

Liberals take credit for a number of reforms to the Constitution, and the way it operates, that have enabled the federal government to help those on the margins of society:
- Liberals have always been strong advocates of extending the right to vote to all Americans and were in the forefront of the campaigns that led to the Nineteenth Amendment (extending the franchise to women), the Twenty-Third Amendment (giving the mainly black residents of Washington DC — a separate district, not a part of any of the 50 states — the right to vote in presidential elections) and the Twenty-Fourth Amendment (abolishing all 'poll taxes' that required people to pay a fee if they wanted to register to vote — a practice used in southern states to limit black participation in elections).
- Similarly, it was liberal judges on the Supreme Court in the 1960s who ruled that the provisions in the Bill of Rights intended to protect criminal suspects had to be applied in ways that were meaningful, for example telling people that they had the right not to testify against themselves (the right to remain silent) when they were arrested.

However, they would have liked to have gone further. In the 1970s, liberals led a movement for an 'equal rights amendment' to the Constitution that would have made sex discrimination unconstitutional. Also, just as the conservatives have welcomed recent Supreme Court judgements, liberals have been alarmed by them.

Centrists and the Constitution

For Americans not on the right or left of the political spectrum, the Constitution is often seen as having shaped the identity and development of their country. To the extent that the USA can be said to be the most powerful nation in the world in economic and military terms and providing the greatest amount of freedom to its inhabitants, it is often the Constitution rather than American politicians that is given the credit. As a result, the Founding Fathers are regarded almost as prophets, and the document they created is treated in ways that religious texts are treated in other societies. As one commentator put it, 'the fact that a constitution was originally a political document is all but forgotten'.

This is not to say that centrists do not see any flaws in the Constitution:
- The lack of political progress that can result from the separation of powers, combined with the system of checks and balances, causes frustration. This was

the case between 2006 and 2008, when the Republicans controlled the executive branch and the Democrats had a majority in both houses of Congress.

- Conversely, at other times the system of checks and balances does not appear to work effectively enough, as when Congress failed to forcefully press the administration of President George W. Bush about the claimed evidence of weapons of mass destruction in Iraq that was used as the justification for massive armed force.
- There are times when the constitutional protections of freedom appear not to work, as when terrorist suspects were detained for years without trial after the attacks of 11 September 2001.

However, there is an abiding faith among centrists that the US political system, operating within the framework of the Constitution, will invariably find the right balance over time:

- To resolve the lack of political direction in the period 2006–08, the public placed the blame on the Republicans and came down firmly on the side of the Democrats in the 2008 elections.
- When the president was able to advance his military plans and attack Iraq, costing the lives of over 4,000 US soldiers and tens of thousands of Iraqis, he paid the price with levels of approval at a record low.
- The detention without trial of 'enemy combatants' was forcefully challenged by the Supreme Court in a series of rulings between 2004 and 2008. (See page 56 for more detail.)

Challenging the Constitution

There is one other viewpoint on the Constitution that is held by a significant minority of Americans. This is the view that when the Founding Fathers forged the 'three-fifths compromise' that allowed slavery to continue, even though the opening words of the Constitution claim that it was created to 'secure the Blessings of Liberty', they gave rise to a political system that permitted people to be treated as inferior on the grounds of race. Furthermore, they believe that the system has continued in this manner ever since — through the era of legalised segregation in the South to the present, with many laws, in practice, discriminating against racial minorities.

According to this view, the Constitution is deeply flawed. It cannot be said to have secured justice and promoted the general welfare, as is claimed in its Preamble, and will not be able to do so for as long as it restricts government from taking large-scale measures (of the kind planned in the Great Society programme) to support those communities on the margins of society.

Conclusion

To be in a position to tackle any questions on this topic, you need to have a strong understanding of:

- the thinking behind the Constitution — what the Founding Fathers aimed to achieve
- how the Constitution works — its key features, such as the system of checks and balances and how it is amended
- the special significance of federalism as a mechanism to limit the power of the federal government — and how it has developed
- the specific rights protected in the Bill of Rights
- the ideological viewpoints on the effectiveness of the Constitution

The final point is especially important for essays. You will *always* be expected to demonstrate different perspectives on issues, as this is how synoptic skills are tested.

The Supreme Court
Guardians of the Constitution

The Constitution is the fundamental law of the USA. That is to say that all laws, at both state and federal levels, have to conform to the Constitution. The same applies to the actions of the people who are responsible for putting laws into effect — the governors at state level and the president at federal level. Any law, or action, that is not faithful to the Constitution is invalid, or unconstitutional.

These simple facts mean that it was clear, even when the Constitution was written, that there would have to be a process for addressing claims that a particular law or action was not constitutional. Yet the Founding Fathers made no provision for such a process.

This omission has great significance. In the system of checks and balances, intended to place limitations on the powers of the three branches of the federal government, the *balance* element is crucial: each branch needs to be strong enough, relative to the other branches, to be able to exert checks. However, the power to interpret the Constitution represents by far the strongest check available to any of the branches. It enables that branch to declare all policies of a certain type to be contrary to the Constitution and, even more significantly, that the Constitution *requires* the implementation of a certain type of policy.

As the Constitution is a legal document, it was logical that any interpretation of how it should be applied to particular situations would be the responsibility of judges, and because the Constitution is the most important legal document in the country, it was logical that it would be the most senior judges who would take on this responsibility. In the absence of guidance from the Founding Fathers, that is what the Supreme Court decided in the landmark case of *Marbury* v *Madison* in 1803 (14 years after the Constitution came into effect).

However, once the Supreme Court had awarded itself the role of guardian of the Constitution, the formidable power of interpreting the Constitution — known as **judicial review** — was in the hands of a small number of unelected people. Considering that the aim of the Founding Fathers when drafting the Constitution was to create a political system that prevented anyone, or any group, from building excessive power and using that power to infringe liberty, some Americans see this situation as highly dangerous and contrary to the spirit of the Constitution. Other Americans disagree, believing that the only people who can be trusted with such immense responsibilities are neutral legal experts with nothing to gain, personally, from their decisions.

Limitations on the judiciary

Judicial review clearly unbalances the system of checks and balances, giving the Supreme Court the greatest power available to any of the branches of government. However, there are some constitutional checks on judicial power:

- A constitutional amendment can overturn a Supreme Court decision. This has happened twice. The Eleventh Amendment (1795) overturned a controversial ruling in the case of *Chisholm* v *Georgia,* and the Sixteenth Amendment (1913) reversed a Supreme Court ruling that had declared a federal income tax to be unconstitutional.
- The Constitution gives Congress the power to alter the number of judges on the Supreme Court. This is not, on the face of it, a check on judicial power but it was used this way in 1937 by President F. D. Roosevelt, who proposed a bill to add up to six extra judges to the Supreme Court in response to a series of rulings striking down his New Deal legislation. The bill was not passed by Congress, but the threat was seen as having the desired effect as the court stopped rejecting the New Deal programmes.

There are also some checks on judicial power that are informal or that occur naturally as a result of the way that the court operates:

- Although judges are not elected, it is said that they 'follow the election returns', meaning that they take note of the way that election results reflect the national mood and, consciously or subconsciously, take this into account in their rulings.
- Judges cannot initiate cases. They can express a view only on cases that come before them, which limits the range of issues their rulings may affect.
- Similarly, the Supreme Court hears only a relatively small number of cases each year. In recent years, it has heard fewer than 100 cases per annum. This also has the effect of limiting the number of issues with potentially political significance that may come before it.

In practice, the last two points do not have a great impact on judicial power, as people or groups with a political agenda (pressure groups) will do all they can to provide the Supreme Court with opportunities to rule on controversial issues, hoping that the court will interpret the Constitution in ways that benefit the interests of those people or groups. To bring a test case to court, a pressure group will put funds and legal expertise behind a court case that challenges a legal principle. For example, in 1954, the civil rights organisation NAACP won the case of *Brown* v *Board of Education, Topeka, Kansas*, which outlawed racial segregation — a ruling that may have had a greater impact on US society than any other pressure group initiative in the twentieth century. (Note: If you can draw on an understanding of the role of pressure groups in relation to the judiciary, a Unit 3C topic, the quality of your analysis will be improved.)

Of greater significance is the fact that the Supreme Court does not have power to enforce its rulings. For this, it is dependent on the executive branch at federal, state and local levels (the president, governors and mayors). If these politicians either refuse to implement the decisions of the court or do so half-heartedly, there is little that the judges can do about it. When the Supreme Court ruled in 1954, in the case of *Brown* v *Board of Education* (see above), that racial segregation in schools was unconstitutional, state governors across the South refused to accept the decision and implement the ruling. The court kept handing down judgements affirming its decision and the South kept defying or evading it (for example by closing the schools). President Eisenhower was reluctant to intervene and use the forces at his disposal to support the Supreme Court (with the famous exception of the army being used to integrate a school in Arkansas), and so only patchy progress was made towards integration for the next 10 years. It took the Civil Rights Act of 1964, which gave the federal government additional power to force the states to comply, to bring to an end the racial segregation that had been declared unconstitutional a decade earlier.

Overall, therefore, there are few effective restrictions on judicial power. With the formal checks being used only in exceptional circumstances, and some of the informal limitations making little impact in reality, the main constraint on judicial power is the extent to which the judges choose to use it in a restrained manner.

Judicial philosophies

Supreme Court judges, like the rest of the population, are sharply divided on how they see their power of judicial review and how it should be used. These divisions centre on the most appropriate role for the judicial branch in the Founding Fathers' constitutional plan and they tend to reflect wider ideological viewpoints on the US political system.

Broadly, judges fall into one of two categories: **judicial restraint** and **judicial activism**.

Judicial restraint

Judges in this category base constitutional interpretation (judicial review) on one simple principle: any decision that prohibits actions (telling people what they cannot do) or compels actions (forcing people do things) ought to be made by people who are subject to effective checks on their powers and who can be held accountable for their decisions.

They see this approach as being consistent with the founding principles of their country. The USA rebelled against British rule in 1776 because of the decision-making process in the UK that allowed one man (the king) to impose his policies on everyone else, knowing that he would not have to suffer any consequences for his actions. The Constitution was designed to ensure that the American people would not have to endure this type of decision making, that inevitably gives rise to tyranny, and two of the constitutional protections against it are the system of checks and balances and the requirement that policy makers are held to account in elections. The checks on the judiciary, however, are limited and rarely used; and federal judges are appointed for life, not elected, and therefore do not have the kind of restraint imposed on them that comes from the knowledge that they can be punished at the polls and removed from office if their decisions prove unpopular with the voters.

Under these circumstances, according to this view, judges should exercise restraint when ruling on an issue that has political implications. Their options should be as follows:

- Refuse to hear the case and refer the issue to be dealt with by Congress, which is designated by the Constitution to be the elected (and therefore accountable) policy-making branch of government. This approach is not often adopted by judges, as demonstrated by the fact that the most famous case of this kind, *Luther* v *Borden,* dates back to 1849.
- Rule that the court should respect laws passed by Congress and the actions of the president, especially in the area of foreign affairs, unless there is an extremely strong constitutional basis for doing otherwise. Famously, the judge regarded as the greatest advocate of judicial restraint, Justice Oliver Wendell Holmes (who served on the Supreme Court from 1902 to 1932), argued that it was his duty as a judge to enforce 'even laws that I believe to embody mistakes'.
- Restrict their rulings only to the legal aspects of the case, not addressing any wider political implications that the case may have. This approach was demonstrated in *Ayotte* v *Planned Parenthood* (2006), a case concerning the highly controversial issue of abortion, when the judgement stated that 'we limit the solution to the problem...we do not revisit our abortion precedents'.

Moreover, when dealing with a case in which judges cannot avoid policy making, the philosophy of judicial restraint provides an approach that they should adopt. Judges should limit their considerations to the precise meaning of the relevant parts of the Constitution and its amendments, together with any evidence of the thinking of those who wrote them.

For example, in the case of *Plessy* v *Ferguson* (1896), the landmark decision that permitted local authorities to segregate people according to their race, the ruling was justified on the basis that when the Fourteenth Amendment (granting ex-slaves rights under the Constitution) was debated in Congress, there was nothing to suggest that equal rights meant racial intermixing, and a number of contributions indicated that Congress did not expect white and black Americans to integrate.

This approach to judicial decision making is called **strict constructionism**.

Judicial activism

Judges in the other category base constitutional interpretation on a different, but equally simple, principle: the rights in the Constitution, especially the Bill of Rights, have to be applied to *everyone* and have to apply in a way that is *meaningful* in each era.

According to this view, there is a clear benefit in unelected judges having responsibility for constitutional interpretation. Elected politicians are prone to neglect the rights of those groups in society who cannot vote. Marginal groups, such as the homeless, criminals and, for most of the nation's history, African-Americans, have been particularly vulnerable to the misuse of power (for example abuse of power by the police). The elected branches have a poor record of providing protection for such groups and have, on many occasions, appealed to prejudice and bigotry to win power or remain in office. Unelected judges do not have to consider popularity in their decision making and are therefore more likely to be true to the spirit of the Constitution, applying it equally to *everyone*, including groups facing hostility from the majority.

Moreover, judicial activists believe that the Constitution has to be applied in ways that are relevant to the modern world. In many respects, this is a straightforward matter: almost everyone agrees that the First Amendment's protection of free speech extends to the use of the telephone and e-mail, even though these did not exist when the Bill of Rights was adopted. In other respects, 'updating' the Constitution can be highly controversial. As social attitudes change, judges may interpret the Constitution in ways that reflect these changes. Although it can be argued that it is the responsibility of elected, accountable, politicians to make such changes through the law, judicial activists assert that the protection of rights according to contemporary standards is too important an issue to wait for politicians to bring the law up to date. The political process can be slow: there may be resistance to change on the part of conservatives, or elected politicians may lack the courage to make changes that could prove electorally unpopular. Making constitutional protections meaningful, therefore, should be the responsibility of judges.

This means that judgements may be based on factors that go beyond consideration of the precise meaning of the words of the Constitution and the thinking of the people who wrote the documents and its amendments. The practical application of the Constitution, in view of changing social attitudes, should also be considered.

For example, in the case of *Brown v Board of Education* (1954), the landmark case that made racial segregation unconstitutional (thereby reversing *Plessy v Ferguson*), advances in psychiatry, demonstrating that segregation made black children believe they were racially inferior, were given more weight than the thinking of the nineteenth-century politicians who had drafted the Fourteenth Amendment without intending equal rights to lead to racial integration.

This approach to judicial decision making is called **loose constructionism**.

Political significance of rival judicial philosophies

Judicially restrained judges

Judges who favour judicial restraint tend to be conservative in outlook. Their rulings are unlikely to lead to change, as they prefer the elected branches to introduce new policies. Their reluctance to 'legislate from the bench' means that on most occasions they will leave the existing social order undisturbed.

The only time when they think it right to alter policy is when, in their judgement, previous rulings have been incorrect and they have the opportunity to reverse them. Such decisions clearly change the way the Constitution is applied, but do so in ways that are intended to be more faithful to its meaning and to the aims of the Founding Fathers than to the rulings that are being reversed. This is seen as **conservative judicial activism**, which serves to return the USA to an earlier golden age. This approach is associated with the New Right tendencies of fiscal conservatism, which deplores the steady growth in the size and scope of the federal government throughout the twentieth century, and social conservatism, which favours a return to the 'family values' of earlier times and resists the agenda of the women's rights and gay rights movements. (Note: If you can draw on an understanding of the main political ideologies, a Unit 3C topic, the quality of your analysis will be improved.)

Judicially active judges

Judges who favour judicial activism tend to be liberal or left wing. Their rulings aim to improve the ways in which the Constitution works in practice, ensuring that rights are effectively applied and that the rights of all sections of the population are protected. This may mean redefining what is meant by the rights in the Constitution and who is entitled to them. It may also mean intervening to protect the rights of those who are not being protected by the elected branches. In both cases, their decisions will often have the effect of creating new policy or overturning the politics of the elected branches.

This approach has led to highly controversial decisions in recent decades that politicians and pressure groups are committed to defending or reversing.

Rights of criminal suspects and convicts

- *Gideon* v *Wainwright* (1963): a ruling that, under the Sixth Amendment, all suspects are entitled to a lawyer to defend them and that the state should provide a defence lawyer if the suspect cannot afford one.
- *Miranda* v *Arizona* (1966): a ruling that, under the Fifth Amendment, all suspects must be informed of their constitutional right not to incriminate themselves by remaining silent when questioned. (Together, these two rulings form the basis of suspects being 'read their rights' by the police on arrest.)
- *Furman* v *Georgia* (1972): a ruling that, under the Eighth Amendment, the death penalty amounted to 'cruel and unusual punishment' and was therefore uncon-stitutional.
- *Gregg* v *Georgia* (1976): a ruling in which, as a result of changes in the methods of execution used, the death penalty was reinstated as constitutional.

The first three of the above cases were welcomed by liberals in the USA, but condemned by conservatives. The fourth, reversing *Furman* v *Georgia*, was celebrated by conservatives.

Abortion

- *Roe* v *Wade* (1973): a ruling that women have a constitutional right to have an abortion, on the grounds that this is a private decision and privacy is protected by the Constitution. As privacy is not mentioned in the Constitution or Bill of Rights, this case has remained a highly controversial example of judicial activism, seen by conservatives as judges imposing their own standards and views on the Constitution in order to liberalise social policy in ways that would not have been achieved through the democratic process.
- *Carhart* v *Gonzales* (2007): a ruling upholding a law banning a specific abortion procedure, known as partial-birth abortion. It was the first such law permitted by the Supreme Court since *Roe* v *Wade* and was seen as a victory for conservatives in their campaign to erode abortion rights and, ultimately, reverse *Roe* v *Wade*.

Civil rights

- *Swann* v *Charlotte-Mecklenburg Board of Education* (1971): a ruling that the school district had done too little to ensure racial integration in its schools. It issued instructions that the fleet of school buses should be used to take black children to the predominantly white school and white children to the school in the mainly African-American district — a policy known as 'bussing'. By not only identifying how constitutional rights had been violated but also specifying the solution to the problem, the court was seen as taking over the role of the legislature, which tradi-tionally has responsibility for changing the law.
- *Milliken* v *Bradley* (1974): a ruling that a bussing plan in the Detroit area was unlawful, effectively undermining the earlier *Swann* v *Charlotte-Mecklenburg* ruling and the policy of bussing in the USA.

Gay rights

- *Lawrence* v *Texas* (2003): a ruling that struck down laws discriminating against homosexuality, celebrated by liberals but raising fears among conservatives that the Supreme Court was moving towards making same-sex marriage a constitutional right.

Appointing federal judges

With Supreme Court rulings having such far-reaching impact, and judicial philosophies playing such a major role in shaping those rulings, the appointment of new judges is one of the most significant events in US politics.

Vacancies

An appointment can only be made when a judge retires or dies in office. In the summer of 2005, there was one retirement and one death within a 5-week period after 11 years with no vacancies occurring.

Nominations

When a vacancy occurs, whoever is president at the time chooses the person to fill the position. Some presidents never have the opportunity to appoint a Supreme Court judge, while others may appoint several: there were no vacancies when Jimmy Carter was president but his successor, Ronald Reagan, appointed four Supreme Court judges. In 2009, President Obama was presented with an opportunity to nominate a Supreme Court judge within 3 months of taking office, following the retirement of Jutice David Souter.

Presidents select judges who, as far as they know, share their political outlook. So, conservative presidents (usually, in recent decades, Republicans) have nominated judges thought to favour judicial restraint and, therefore, to be unlikely to extend constitutional rights, while liberal presidents (usually Democrats) have selected judicial activists expected to protect the interests of the weak and vulnerable. However, their choices have not always behaved as expected once they have joined the court. The most active court in recent history was led by Chief Justice Earl Warren, who was appointed by President Eisenhower in the expectation that Warren would adopt a conservative approach (in line with his record before his appointment).

Because judges can be unpredictable, presidents have become increasingly careful to vet candidates before offering them the position. The president's staff research the judgements, writings and speeches of the potential nominees in depth and interview them at length.

Confirmations

After the public announcement of a nominee, the Senate holds hearings to assess his or her suitability. Other political activists, from political parties and pressure groups, also get involved in the process, mounting campaigns for or against the nomination. Any personal or professional failings are likely to be exposed and publicised by this process, but the main focus is on the judicial philosophy of the nominee. If the nominee is perceived to be at the extreme range of either judicial philosophy, his or her suitability to serve on the nation's highest court will be called into question. For example, when President Reagan nominated Robert Bork, who had been a critic of judicial activism since the 1930s, the public campaign against him, combined with a poor performance in the public hearings before the Senate, undermined his standing and he was not confirmed. Since then, every confirmation hearing has been accompanied by political campaigning, with pressure groups spending millions of dollars in support of or in opposition to nominees.

If the nominee successfully negotiates this process, and the Senate votes to confirm the appointment by a simple majority, the person is appointed to the Supreme Court.

The Roberts Court (2005–)

What was the balance between judicial activism and judicial restraint in the Supreme Court in the early months of Barack Obama's presidency in 2009? Six of the nine justices had been appointed by Republican presidents. This would suggest a conservative majority, with the court's rulings characterised by judicial restraint. However, the picture is more complex.

- Two of the justices have been seen by most analysts as conservative judicial activists: Antonin Scalia, appointed by President Reagan (Republican), and Clarence Thomas, appointed by President George Bush Snr (Republican).
- Two favour judicial restraint: Chief Justice John Roberts and Samuel Alito, both appointed by President George Bush Jr (Republican).
- Four favour judicial activism. Two of these were appointed by President Clinton (Democrat): Ruth Bader-Ginsberg and Steven Breyer. One was appointed by President Obama (Democrat): Sonia Sotomayor. The other is an example of a judge appointed by a Republican president to be a restrained justice but then turned out to be an activist. John Paul Stevens was appointed by President Ford.
- With an even balance between judicial restraint and judicial activism in the Supreme Court, the key vote is usually cast by the 'swing judge', whose decisions fluctuate between the two camps. Anthony Kennedy, appointed by President Reagan, has been in the majority in most major judgements in recent years. This situation is unlikely to change during the Obama presidency, as it is anticipated that any further retirements will be from the liberal wing of the court and will be replaced with like-minded justices.

Conclusion

To be in a position to tackle any questions on this topic, you need to have a strong understanding of:

- the significance of judicial review
- how the power of judicial review can be used:

- judicial restraint, the justification for this viewpoint and the strict constructionist approach to judicial rulings
- judicial activism, the justification for this viewpoint and the loose constructionist approach to judicial rulings
- the political implications of the two approaches to judicial decision making
- the political character of the appointment process
- the political balance on the Roberts Court at the start of Barack Obama's presidency

The ability to weigh up the strengths and weaknesses of the rival approaches to judicial review is especially important for essays. You will *always* be expected to demonstrate different perspectives on issues, as this is how synoptic skills are tested.

Congress

The importance of Congress

When the USA broke away from the UK in 1776, the first system of government consisted *only* of a legislature. The Articles of Confederation provided America with no executive or judiciary because it was thought that policies should be decided collectively and then implemented by the 13 individual states. This was intended to ensure that no monarch-like figure could emerge.

This system of government proved inadequate to meet the challenges facing the young country and was replaced by the current system devised at the Philadelphia Convention in 1787. However, even in the revised system, there was an intention that policy would be made collectively to avoid the emergence of a monarch-like figure. Congress was therefore expected to be the most important and most powerful branch of government. This section of the guide examines the work of Congress and the extent to which, in the twenty-first century, it meets the expectations of the Founding Fathers.

A bicameral legislature

The expectation that Congress would be the most powerful branch of government led to an addition to the system of separation of powers and checks and balances — the powers of the legislature were divided between two chambers, with each monitoring how the other used its powers:
- **The House of Representatives**, whose members face re-election every 2 years, was given primary responsibility for managing the economy. All proposals involving the raising of tax or how those taxes are spent have to be considered by the House first. Few issues matter more to people than part of their income

being taken by the government, especially if they feel that the government is not spending the money wisely or appropriately, and giving the House of Representatives this responsibility meant that people could hold politicians to account on a frequent basis for the use of their money.
* **The Senate**, whose members face re-election every 6 years, was given primary responsibility for long-term issues such as monitoring executive decisions that have lasting consequences, for example treaties with other countries and appointments to senior positions such as the Supreme Court.

General legislation was the responsibility of both houses, with each having the ability to put forward legislative proposals and with each separately examining those proposals.

The executive branch, not the legislative branch, was expected to take the lead in foreign affairs. Apart from that, its only role was to implement the decisions of Congress.

Roles of Congress

From this original design, the following congressional roles have developed:
* **Legislative.** The two houses of Congress have joint responsibility for passing federal legislation.
* **Scrutiny.** Both houses of Congress are responsible for monitoring how the laws they have passed are implemented by the government departments that make up the executive branch. Both may also investigate any abuse of power by those in the other two branches of the federal government and have a constitutional procedure for removing them from office if necessary (impeachment). They have joint responsibility for authorising the most serious form of military action — going to war. The Senate has the additional responsibility of scrutinising treaties signed by the president and appointments made by the president.
* **Representation.** Each person elected to Congress has a responsibility to promote the best interests of the voters who chose them (and who have the option of choosing someone else at the next election).

As with other legislatures around the world, some of these roles may place contradictory demands on Congress. In particular, what is in the best interests of the nation may not be in the best interests of the state or district of individual members of Congress. For example, when the Cold War ended in the late 1980s, the demands on the armed forces changed and some military bases were no longer needed. While this was good for the country, as it reduced the cost of the armed services, it was not good for those regions that depended heavily on military contracts for employment.

How well does Congress carry out its roles and how well does it manage the sometimes contradictory demands they create? We examine these issues below.

Legislative role of Congress

The Founding Fathers expected Congress to be responsible for each phase of the legislative process, from putting forward proposals, to drafting laws, to passing new laws. The executive branch's role was expected to be limited to implementing those laws, under the watchful eye of Congress to ensure that they were put into effect as the law makers intended. However, the Founding Fathers also inserted a clause in the Constitution that provided an opportunity for the president to 'from time to time give to Congress Information on the State of the Union and recommend to their Consideration such Measures as he shall judge necessary and expedient'.

Since it is extremely difficult for a large group of people, with diverse interests, to develop proposals that take the country forward in a clear direction, and since the Constitution provides the president with an opportunity to play this role, in practice it is the executive branch that has taken over primary responsibility for proposing major legislation. Even in these circumstances, however, Congress will take the initiative on an important issue if there is a sense that the president is failing to do so.

Once draft legislation (a bill) is introduced to Congress, the legislature takes full responsibility for examining and amending it before it can become law and will not hesitate to hold it up or block it if the bill does not meet with its approval.

The legislative process has several phases, outlined below.

The pre-legislative phase (proposals)

The political agenda for the year is set by the president in the State of the Union Address each January, when he outlines the main issues to be dealt with over the following 12 months. Based on these proposals, the executive branch will submit a budget for the year and then begin to put forward bills for the consideration of Congress. Other issues will almost certainly arise as the year progresses, leading to the president submitting further bills.

With only a year to complete work on this package before the next State of the Union Address, there is little time for other proposals from members of Congress to be considered. Despite this, they will put forward bills of their own, often related to the main issues of their district or state. In addition, members of Congress will periodically act together to propose national legislation on a controversial matter that has not been included in the presidential initiative. For example, in 2006 Congress threatened to pass a law to block the takeover of several US ports by a firm owned by the government of Dubai on the grounds that it threatened national security. The president, arguing that Dubai was an ally of the USA, supported the deal. Nevertheless, with public opinion hostile to the takeover, Congress moved forward with legislation. It was only halted when the firm announced its intention to sell the ports to another company.

The committee stage

Legislatures debate whether they agree in principle with a bill and then, if they support its overall purpose, examine the detailed provisions to ensure that it will effectively achieve its aims. In many legislatures, these two activities are conducted separately. In the UK, for example, Parliament debates the principles of a bill first (the second reading) and then examines the detailed provisions afterwards (the committee stage).

When legislation is introduced into either house of Congress, it is referred to a committee, which examines both the overall aims of the bill as well as its detailed provisions. This puts tremendous power in the hands of committees and, especially, the chairperson of each committee.

The chairperson is always from the party with the most seats in the relevant chamber and is usually the person who has been the longest serving member of the committee. If the chairperson decides not to schedule the bill for discussion by the committee, he or she is said to have **pigeon-holed** the bill and it can make no further progress. As bills can only become law if they pass through both houses of Congress, pigeon-holing means that the bill has been killed. By tradition, this is not done with presidential proposals but it happens quite frequently with initiatives that have come from other members of their chamber.

The chairperson may decide to block a bill's progress for a range of reasons:
- **Ideological considerations.** A left-wing Democratic chairperson is unlikely to agree with a bill put forward by a conservative Republican.
- **Personal considerations.** A chairperson may block a bill proposed by someone he or she personally dislikes or as a result of a political battle fought in the past.
- **District/state considerations.** A chairperson may judge a bill to be contrary to the interests of his or her constituents.

If a bill meets with the approval of the committee chairperson, it then faces the obstacle of debate among the committee members. The majority of committee members, like the chairperson, will be from the party with the most seats in the chamber.

As well as discussing the bill among its own members, the committee will hold 'hearings' in which experts and representatives of pressure groups have the opportunity to express their views on any aspect of the bill. As a result of these sessions, amendments may be proposed and adopted. At this stage, ideological, personal and constituency issues will also play a role.

Any amendments that are designed to benefit a member's constituency directly are known as **earmarks**. When a bill is substantially amended by many members in this way, the process is referred to as **pork-barrel** politics. Members of Congress may, on occasion, make reciprocal deals with their colleagues in which they support each other's earmarks, a process known as **log-rolling**.

If the bill, with amendments, meets with the approval of a majority of the committee members, they will vote for it to go forward to be debated by the full chamber.

Debate by the full chamber

At this stage, the procedures in the House of Representatives and the Senate differ significantly:

- In the House of Representatives, the progress of a bill that has survived the committee stage will be affected by the decisions of the House Rules Committee. This committee can decide when (or whether) to schedule the debate, the length of the debate and the rules that will apply to the debate. If it decides to debate the bill under the closed rule, no further amendments may be made at this stage. However, if the bill is debated under the open rule, with the possibility of amendments, the ideological, personal and constituency concerns of all 435 members of the house can be brought to bear on its provisions and it can be altered out of all recognition. At the end of this process, if a majority votes in favour of the bill, it will have successfully negotiated the House of Representatives.

- In the Senate, there is a tradition of unrestricted debate on measures that come out of committee. Here the procedures are designed to ensure that the interests of states with small populations are protected. An individual Senator or a group of Senators working together can use a device known as a **filibuster** to block the progress of a bill by keeping the debate going and stopping a vote from being called. It takes a special motion — a **cloture**, requiring 60 votes — to end a filibuster. This means that a bill is not assured of passing the Senate even if it has the support of the majority (over 50) of the Senators. A bill needs a filibuster-proof majority of 60 to be certain of passing.

Conference Committee

Bills that pass through both chambers of Congress have almost always been amended in different ways. However, only one version of a bill can be presented to the president to be signed into law. Therefore, the different versions have to be harmonised. This is done by representatives of each chamber meeting to negotiate an agreed version.

It is possible for a bill to get stuck in Conference Committee if the representatives cannot reach agreement, and even if they do produce a joint version it is possible for one of the chambers to vote against it. So even at this stage it is possible for a bill to fail.

Veto

The final hurdle that a bill has to negotiate is a presidential veto. If the president decides to veto a bill, it can still become law if the veto is overridden with a two-thirds majority in both chambers of Congress. This invariably requires the support of members of both parties in both chambers — a threshold that is difficult, but not impossible, to reach.

Scrutiny role of Congress

Congressional scrutiny serves five purposes:

- to judge the suitability of people chosen by the president to high office in the executive or judicial branches

- to monitor how laws are being implemented, and to hold the relevant people in the executive branch to account if there is evidence of this not being done properly
- to investigate any suggestions of abuse of power by people holding high office
- to examine agreements with other countries made by the president on behalf of the USA
- to act as a check on the president's use of armed force against other countries

Congressional scrutiny fulfils these purposes in several ways.

Confirming presidential nominees

This is a task assigned by the Constitution to the Senate. Whenever the president nominates someone to fill a senior federal position, such as a Supreme Court judge or the head of one of the government's departments, the Senate has to agree to the decision. This is done by a simple majority, with more than half the Senators voting in favour. Before the vote, hearings will be held in which the nominee, relevant experts and other groups with an interest in the outcome will be questioned.

In most cases, this results in the Senate giving a wholehearted endorsement of the nominee. In a few cases, however, the Senate will vote against confirming the president's choice, as for example with Robert Bork, nominated to the Supreme Court in 1987 by President Reagan. More commonly, the hearings process will lead to revelations that cause the nominee to withdraw his or her name. When President George Bush Jr nominated Harriet Miers to the Supreme Court in 2005, the perception that she lacked the necessary experience and ability led to her withdrawal. Similarly, when President Obama nominated former Senator Tom Daschle to head the Department of Health, it was revealed that he had not paid all his taxes and he too withdrew.

If it becomes apparent during the hearings that a candidate lacks the support in the Senate needed for confirmation, there is a loophole in the process that allows a president to make the appointment without the agreement of the Senate. Whenever the Senate breaks for a holiday, the Constitution allows the president to make a **recess appointment** (a provision needed in the days before modern transport systems, when Congress was away from the capital city for weeks at a time). Whoever is appointed in this situation can occupy the position until the end of the Senate session. As each session lasts for 2 years, recess appointees can hold an important office for an extended period without having been confirmed. At the beginning of the following session, however, the office holder must either resign or face a renewed confirmation process. Unsurprisingly, the Senate, having earlier been circumvented, is rarely sympathetic to recess appointees and in most cases they are not confirmed.

Committee monitoring of government departments

The committees that examine legislation also monitor how that legislation is implemented. They seek to ensure that it is done efficiently and that any indications of incompetence are addressed. They also seek to ensure that legislation is put into effect not only in line with the letter of the law but also in the spirit of the law. This has become more important in recent years with the increasing number of 'signing statements', in which the president signs a bill into law but at the same time announces that he does not intend to put much effort into implementing aspects that he does not agree with.

Committees respond to any reports, often from the press or 'whistleblowers', that a government department's performance is a cause for concern. They will call for any relevant documents to be produced and hold hearings at which people connected with the reports may be questioned. For example, in 2007, hearings into the dismissal of nine senior lawyers by the Attorney General led to his resignation. Alberto Gonzales, appointed by President George Bush Jr, had been accused of dismissing the lawyers because they were not supporters of the Republican Party, and his testimony at the hearings failed to convince members of Congress that the matter had been dealt with properly.

Finally, the committees are responsible for monitoring how the federal departments spend the funds allocated by Congress. They may question whether departmental funding priorities are faithful to the intent behind the allocation and, if they feel that funds are not being spent appropriately, will make specific provision for money to be allocated to projects they support.

Investigations and impeachment

The type of hearing that led to the resignation of Alberto Gonzales can develop into a full-scale investigation. This is what happened to President Bill Clinton, following allegations of inappropriate conduct. The investigation started with claims of corrupt financial deals before he became president but ended with claims that he had had a sexual relationship with a woman working at the White House and had lied about it under oath.

Anyone holding high office in the federal government who is accused of abusing his or her position, being grossly incompetent or behaving in a way that brings his or her office into disrepute can be put through a trial procedure that can lead to his or her dismissal. This process is called **impeachment**.

It is the constitutional responsibility of the House of Representatives to decide whether to start this process. The members vote by a simple majority to bring articles of impeachment against the accused person (the equivalent of charging someone in a criminal matter). This will lead to an impeachment trial in the Senate. The case against the accused is made by a delegation from the House of Representatives. The accused has to defend himself or herself. The Chief Justice of the Supreme Court presides over the proceedings, and the Senate decides on whether or not the case has been proved. A two-thirds majority of the Senators is required for the accused person to be found guilty of the charges and removed from office. Only two presidents have ever gone through the impeachment process: Andrew Johnson in 1868 and Bill Clinton in 1998.

Neither was found guilty. (President Richard Nixon resigned at the height of the Watergate scandal before impeachment proceedings began.)

Ratification of treaties

This is a task assigned by the Constitution to the Senate. Any formal treaty, entering into an agreement with one or more other countries, must be scrutinised and voted on by the Senate. A two-thirds majority is required.

As with confirmations, most such treaties receive the wholehearted support of the Senate, but there have been some high-profile exceptions. The Treaty of Versailles (1919), bringing the First World War to an end, was rejected; the Senate refused to ratify SALT II (1979), a treaty that aimed to reduce the rate at which nuclear weapons were being built and deployed; and the Senate also refused to ratify the Comprehensive Test Ban Treaty in 1999.

In another parallel with confirmations, presidents have a loophole available to them that can be used if there appears to be insufficient support in the Senate for a proposed treaty. They can sign an **executive agreement**. These have the same status in international law as treaties but, because they are not mentioned in the Constitution, they are not subject to a two-thirds majority in a Senate vote. A simple majority in both chambers is sufficient.

Declaration of war

This responsibility is assigned to both chambers in Congress. When the Constitution was written, the main mode of global transport was sailing ships. The USA was therefore many weeks away from its potential enemies in Europe. The president was given the role of commander-in-chief, able to send armed forces into action if the USA was attacked, but if a full-scale war was looming it was Congress that was supposed to make the decision as to whether or not to continue down this path.

In modern times, fighting can and often does erupt quickly and, once a conflict has begun, countries rarely formally declare war. The last time Congress declared war was the day after the attack on Pearl Harbor at the start of the Second World War. Consequently, this check on the way in which the president uses armed force has effectively fallen into disuse.

There have been attempts to restore the position of Congress, through the War Powers Resolution passed in 1973 and through threats to withhold funds unless the president responds to congressional concerns, but neither has been successful. Members of Congress have been reluctant to invoke the War Powers Resolution, which provides for US forces to be pulled out of conflicts that Congress has not approved, in case they appear unpatriotic. Similarly, when the Democrats gained control of Congress in 2006 and attempted to force President Bush Jr to announce a timetable for withdrawal from Iraq by threatening to withhold funds for the war, they quickly backed down when he called their bluff.

Representative role of Congress

Members of Congress are expected to look after the interests of the people who voted them into office and whom they will have to face in the next election. Unless they are seen to have served their area well, they are likely to face a strong challenge and could lose their seats. Conversely, if they are seen to have provided a good service to their constituents, they may not face any challengers at all and be returned unopposed.

Members of Congress are judged according to certain criteria.

Casework

Any constituent who approaches a member of Congress with a concern or a problem that needs to be solved is unlikely to be turned away, even if the issue is not a federal matter and ought to be addressed by a state or local official. These approaches will be handled by a staff member and treated as a priority until resolved. Members of Congress operate on the principle that any help they give, or any failure to help an individual, will be mentioned to at least 20 other people and influence the way all those people vote.

Earmarks

Members of Congress want to be able to demonstrate at each election that their time in Washington DC has directly benefited their area in terms of federal resources. They aim to show that they are responsible for laws, or have added provisions to laws, that have led to practical improvements in people's lives (such as a new transport system) or have created new jobs (such as research projects). Therefore they will seek to have such projects added to legislation as it passes through Congress. Those on key committees, especially those who chair committees, are in a particularly strong position to do this.

Active participation in local events

Constituents also like to know that their representatives in Congress continue to be the kind of person they can relate to. At elections it is a common accusation of challengers that politicians have been seduced by the high life in Washington DC and have lost touch with the concerns of ordinary people. This line of argument can be particularly effective in areas far away from the capital, where the work and lifestyles of federal politicians seem remote. To guard against such attacks, members of Congress make frequent visits to their home areas, attending high-profile events and meeting ordinary voters.

Ideology

A significant proportion of members of Congress represent a district or state with a distinctly right-wing or left-wing electorate. As much as these constituents want their personal and collective interests promoted by their representatives, they also want to see their members of Congress taking a stand on political issues that matter to them. Thus, in some cases, the ideological position of the member of Congress may affect his or her chances of re-election.

The importance of political parties

The review of how Congress operates has made little mention of the role of political parties in the legislature. Political parties, however, have always been a significant factor and have grown in importance in recent decades.

Ideology is identified above as one factor in the decision of committee chairpersons on whether or not to allow a bill to be considered by a committee (pigeon-holing) and in the relationship between members of Congress and their constituents. Party considerations are also significant in virtually every other aspect of the work of Congress

The Speaker

In the House of Representatives, the most important figure is the Speaker. This position goes to the person elected by the Congressmen from the majority party to lead them.

All three Speakers since 1994 have been a person with a clear ideological standpoint:
- Newt Gingrich, who led the Republican Party to victory in the 1994 mid-term elections, was a highly committed conservative, dedicated to defeating the political agenda of the Democratic president, Bill Clinton. Together with his second in-command, Tom DeLay (nicknamed 'The Hammer'), he worked to ensure that all Republicans voted together on issues with ideological significance and blocked the appointment of anyone to the position of committee chairperson if he or she was seen as too accommodating to the Democrats.
- Dennis Hastert, who took over from Gingrich in 1998, operated a policy of ensuring that there was always a 'majority of the majority' when legislation passed through the House of Representatives. This meant that all successful legislation had to have the support of most of the Republican Congressmen, so that the Democrats could not take credit for the success. He also blocked the appointment of committee chairpersons who were not seen as sufficiently loyal to the party.
- Nancy Pelosi became the first woman to hold the position of Speaker, when the Democrats gained control of the House of Representatives following the 2006 congressional elections. Regarded as the most left-wing member of the house, she has been seen as having a liberal ideological agenda in a reverse image of that of Newt Gingrich. However, she leads a less united party than her two Republican predecessors and there has been a perception that the highly ideological approach of the Republican Party between 1994 and 2006 contributed to its eventual downfall, so the Democrats in Congress have been somewhat less partisan than the Republicans.

Control of congressional committees

The party with the most seats in each chamber of Congress has a majority on each committee. This means that if an issue creates divisions along ideological lines, the party with the majority can force through or block the initiative. The majority party also controls all the committee chairmanships, and these have increasingly gone to people on ideological grounds.

Votes by the full chamber

Since 1994, whenever legislation has reached the floor of the chamber, votes have tended to be cast along party lines. When President Obama, in 2009, attempted to secure bipartisan support for his stimulus bill to boost the economy to combat the economic recession, he invited leaders of the Republican Party from both the House of Representatives and the Senate to discuss the bill's provisions and offered to make amendments in order to win their support. Despite this, every Republican in the House of Representatives voted against the bill and only three Republicans in the Senate voted for it.

Oversight of the executive

The extent to which congressional committees probe into the operation of executive departments, and publish embarrassing revelations, depends on whether the party in control of Congress is the same as the party controlling the White House. During the final 2 years of the presidency of George W. Bush, when the Democrats were in control of both houses of Congress, his administration faced far more intense scrutiny than during the first 6 years, when the Republicans were in the majority in Congress. For example, a congressional investigation in 2007 into the sacking of lawyers in the Justice Department because they were not Republicans led to the resignation of the Attorney General, Alberto Gonzales.

Investigations and impeachment

The aggressive approach to oversight by the Democrats between 2006 and 2008 was more than matched by the earlier investigations mounted by Republicans in Congress into the financial and personal affairs of President Bill Clinton, which eventually led to his impeachment over his conduct in relation to his affair with White House intern Monica Lewinsky. When Congress came to vote on the matter, only five Democrats in the House of Representatives voted for the president to be brought to trial in the Senate and no Democratic Senators voted for him to be convicted.

Foreign affairs

Ideology tends to play a smaller role in foreign affairs than in domestic matters, but it can still be significant. When the Senate refused to ratify the Comprehensive Test Ban Treaty, the vote was largely on party lines, with only five Republicans supporting the treaty. Similarly, when Congress attached a timetable for withdrawal from Iraq to a bill providing funding for the war in 2007, only one Republican Senator voted in favour and only two Democrats voted against.

Pressures on members of Congress

In carrying out their responsibilities, members of Congress have a range of factors to consider — some of which conflict with each other:

- Most members want, above all, to be re-elected. For this to happen, they have to satisfy their constituents that they are serving their interests well in Washington DC. This may mean putting the interests of the area they represent above the interests of the nation as a whole. Hence the tendency of members to attach earmarks to bills that appear likely to pass into law.
- Many also want to build a career in Congress, which means rising to the higher levels of their party and being put in charge of a congressional committee (if their party has a majority of seats). This may mean demonstrating loyalty to their party, which may, at times, conflict with the interests of their constituents.
- A significant proportion of members of Congress enter politics not only to make a contribution to their community but also because of a commitment to a set of ideas and values (ideology). In some cases, therefore, the top priority of a member of Congress may be to advance a cause or broad political agenda, persuading other members of his or her party to support it. This factor appears to have grown in importance since the early 1990s when the Republican Party's congressional election manifesto, 'Contract with America', swept the party to power in both houses of Congress and put all those elected in a position of having to support the conservative aims of the 'Contract', including elements that they questioned or that appeared to conflict with the interests of their constituency.
- Some of the responsibilities of Congress (especially those of the Senate) require a national or international perspective, such as the efficiency of government departments or the ratification of treaties. In these matters, the constituents may not have strong views, the political parties may be broadly in agreement and there may not be much benefit in terms of career advancement. Under such circumstances, the personal opinion or judgement of the members of Congress may be the most significant factor in reaching decisions.

Finding the right balance between these pressures determines both the way in which members of Congress vote and the development of their careers.

Overall assessment of Congress

The Founding Fathers expected the legislature to take primary responsibility for devising federal policy, based on the close links between ordinary citizens and their elected representatives. Clearly this has not been the case. The president has become the 'chief legislator'. However, members of Congress do play a significant subsidiary role in this respect, as demonstrated for example by the response to the takeover of US ports by a Dubai-based company.

In its other roles, of passing legislation, scrutiny and representation, there are both negative and positive aspects of the way in which Congress carries out its duties.

Legislation

The legislation process is often slow, difficult for ordinary people to understand and results in a substantial proportion of bills failing to pass. It also puts a tremendous amount of power in the hands of committee chairpersons, which would appear to run counter to the aims of the Constitution. Even the bills that do manage to negotiate all the hurdles successfully tend to have many earmarks attached to them that may have little to do with the main purpose of the legislation.

However, on the positive side, the process guarantees that proposed laws coming from the executive branch will be thoroughly examined: there is less chance than in many other countries of the executive getting all the legislation it wants without having to be concerned about the impact of the legislature. Also, as members of Congress can build a career in the legislature, rising to become powerful committee chairs, they tend to specialise in specific policy areas and develop high levels of expertise, which aids their examination of legislative proposals. Finally, there are many Americans who favour small government and believe that it would be unhealthy for all legislation to pass, thus turning the low success rate of bills into an advantage.

Scrutiny

Congress has a range of ways in which it scrutinises the executive branch, from examining the credentials of people who are nominated for high office, to monitoring how well they perform in their leadership positions, to having a say over the final decisions of the president in foreign affairs.

However, with several forms of scrutiny, the executive appears to have found loopholes or exploited weaknesses in the system, calling into question their effectiveness.

Representation

Members of Congress have an impressive record of actively representing the interests of their constituents, working to resolve individual issues and providing improvements for the whole community.

However, this emphasis on local interests can be at the expense of the national interest, and Congress is constantly criticised for its tendency to engage in 'pork-barrel politics' as a result of the determination of its members to add earmarks to bills that are likely to pass.

Conclusion

To be in a position to tackle any questions on this topic, you need to have a strong understanding of:

- the three main roles of Congress
- how Congress carries out these roles
- the strengths and weaknesses of Congress
- the extent to which Congress fulfils the objectives of the Founding Fathers

The ability to weigh up the strengths and weaknesses of Congress is especially important for essays. You will *always* be expected to demonstrate different perspectives on issues, as this is how synoptic skills are tested.

The presidency

An American monarch?

Ensuring that the people of the USA would never suffer oppression at the hands of a powerful, unrestrained leader was the central aim of the Founding Fathers when they produced the Constitution. Yet in modern times, the president of the USA has been routinely described as the most powerful person in the world. This would suggest that the primary objective of the US constitutional system has not been met.

However, prominent American political scientist Richard Neustadt (who specialises in the US presidency and has been an advisor to several presidents) has argued that presidents are so constrained by the system of checks and balances that they have only 'the power to persuade'.

Which is the more accurate characterisation? This part of the guide examines the work of the executive branch of government to provide you with the material to reach an informed judgement.

Roles of the president

The Constitution confers specific powers on the president:

- He is commander-in-chief of the armed services, but cannot declare war.
- He negotiates and signs treaties with other countries, although they must be ratified by the Senate before taking effect.
- He is in charge of diplomatic relations with other countries.
- He has the power to issue pardons to anyone convicted of a crime.

These duties are carried out in most countries by the head of state, so the president carries this title although this is not specified in the Constitution.

The Constitution also confers the following two powers on the president:
- He is responsible for appointing people to head government departments, subject to confirmation by the Senate.
- He can call Congress back into session during a break (recess) at times of national emergency.

These duties are carried out in most countries by the head of government, so the president carries this title although again this is not specified in the Constitution.

In addition, as specified in a clause in the Constitution, the president shall 'from time to time give to Congress Information on the State of the Union and recommend to their Consideration such Measures as he shall judge necessary and expedient'. As the State of the Union Address is delivered annually at the end of January, the president takes a leading role in shaping national policy for the year.

The president also has the power to veto (block) bills that have been passed by Congress. This power is found in Article 1, section 7 of the Constitution.

Otherwise, the Constitution gives the president the broad responsibility of ensuring that the laws of the USA are 'faithfully executed'.

From these constitutional origins, the following presidential roles have developed:
- chief legislator: proposing federal law
- head of government: overseeing the implementation of federal law
- chief diplomat
- commander-in-chief
- head of state
- party leader

Below, we look at how these roles are carried out and how much power they confer on the president.

Chief legislator

The role of the president in proposing legislation is outlined above in the section on the legislative role of Congress. It can be summarised as the president having a more substantial role in initiating legislation than the Founding Fathers anticipated, by virtue of having primary responsibility for proposing major legislation in the State of the Union Address (delivered each January) and proposing the budget (sent to Congress each February), but having little control over the passage of bills once they have been presented to Congress. The check exerted by Congress on the president's legislative role is, therefore, significant.

However, the president does have two weapons at his disposal while legislation is making its way through Congress:

- **Veto.** After all the work that Congress has put into the passage of a bill, the members of the House of Representatives and the Senate do not want the final legislation to be blocked by the president. Therefore, the president is in a strong position to negotiate if there are some aspects of a bill that he would like to see changed. If Congress believes that the president is willing to veto a bill that has not taken his concerns into account, with all its efforts wasted, the legislature is likely to make the changes the president wants. If, however, Congress thinks the president is bluffing, it may refuse to alter the bill. In this game of legislative poker, there is another factor for both sides to consider. If the president is not bluffing and vetoes the bill, does Congress have sufficient support in both chambers (two thirds) to override the veto? If it appears that there is sufficient support, the hand of Congress is strengthened and the president's negotiating position is weakened.
- **Pocket veto.** The president may choose not to engage in a high profile contest with Congress when presented with a bill late in the year. With the complexity and slow pace of the legislative process, it is often the case that there is a rush to complete bills just before Congress goes into recess around Thanksgiving or Christmas (late November or December). Once Congress has closed its session for the year, any bill that has not been signed into law within 10 days dies. This is known as the 'pocket veto'. The bill is not sent back to Congress and therefore cannot be overridden, making the prospect of a pocket veto a particularly effective negotiating tool for the president.

Head of government

Once a bill is passed into law, the president is responsible for its implementation, even if he does not agree with aspects of it.

In recent years, presidents have made increasing use of **signing statements**, in which they announce an intention to apply the new laws selectively, putting little effort into applying those parts with which they disagree. President George Bush Jr made the most extensive use of this device, expressing objections to over 100 bills as he signed them into law.

The practical implementation of the law is done mainly by the 15 executive departments, which, together with a range of other government agencies such as the Federal Reserve (the central bank), are collectively known as the **federal bureaucracy**. The heads (secretaries) of the 15 main departments make up the **cabinet**.

Presidents often find it difficult to get the cabinet to work together as a team to support them in the development of policy, and individual members of cabinet cannot always be relied upon to implement the president's agenda in their departments. There are several reasons for these difficulties:

- The president does not have complete freedom of choice over whom to appoint to the cabinet. It is expected that the group of people who govern America will reflect the diversity of Americans. Therefore, presidents need to fill the 15 cabinet positions with women as well as men, ethnic minorities and people from all regions of the country. The first cabinet of President Obama included two Hispanics, two African-Americans, one Chinese and five women. All regions of the country were represented. He also included two Republicans.

- Even when the above considerations are taken into account, the president may face difficulty in appointing his preferred choices for specific cabinet positions. Some may not accept the offer of a post, either because of existing commitments or because government positions often pay far less than private-sector employment. Others, as we have seen, may not get through the confirmation process.

- Once cabinet members take up their positions, they will be subject to considerable pressure from career civil servants not to abandon projects and policies that have been in place for many years — sometimes decades. As a result, there is a tendency for the heads of departments to drift away from the president's policy agenda over time.

- Even if this does not happen, other departmental pressures may obstruct the implementation of the president's programme. Senior civil servants, who work in the government departments, may have long-term projects that do not have the support of the president and may be willing to work with groups who do support their priorities. They may forge strong alliances with pressure groups that have similar objectives and, if these two groups are joined by key members of congressional committees, who fund the work of the executive branch, an **iron triangle** is formed. This can thwart the will of the president by implementing programmes in ways that conflict with his intentions.

To overcome these obstacles to the delivery of his programme, the president can use the spoils system and the Executive Office of the Presidency (EOP).

The **spoils system** enables the president to appoint political allies to the federal bureaucracy, where they monitor the extent to which civil servants are implementing programmes in ways that are consistent with the president's political priorities.

Executive Office of the Presidency

As government grew throughout the twentieth century, and especially since the New Deal of the 1930s, it became apparent that the president needed support to supervise the bureaucracy. As a result, the **Executive Office of the Presidency** (EOP) was established. Its purpose is to ensure that the president is in a position to make 'responsible decisions, and then when decisions have been made, to assist him in seeing to it that every administrative department and agency is properly informed'.

Its primary responsibilities are:
- preparing the budget (which is done by the Office of Management and Budget)
- planning long-term economic strategies (which is done by the Council of Economic Advisors)
- coordinating the country's diplomatic and military policies (which is done by the National Security Council)

- running the White House Office, where the president's advisors work with him to develop the administration's political strategies, provide advice on response to emergencies, present the president's proposals to the American people and the wider world, liaise and negotiate with Congress and provide a link between the White House and the government departments

The EOP is led by people whose loyalty to the president is unquestioned. Often they have a longstanding relationship with the president, having been close to him for many years even before he decided to run for election to the position. The top advisors to President Bush Jr, such as Karl Rove, worked with him in Texas, while President Obama and his chief of staff, Rahm Emmanuel, are both from Illinois. In addition, most do not have to be confirmed by the Senate and they are not subject to congressional committee monitoring. The president often has greater confidence that his agenda will be advanced by the EOP than by the cabinet and relies on the EOP to ensure that government departments implement the law in ways that are consistent with his overall aims and objectives.

Chief diplomat

Diplomatic relations with other countries are mainly conducted through the State Department, under the leadership of the secretary of state. The appointment of the secretary of state is therefore one of the most important appointments that the president makes: if other countries are not confident that the secretary of state speaks for the president, then diplomatic negotiations are likely to be unfruitful.

When there is a major agreement to be signed, the president becomes directly involved in the process. However, any treaties that are negotiated by the president's administration have to be ratified by the Senate. Often this does not present a problem for the president, but the Senate has rejected some important agreements. Thus, presidents often use a loophole in international law — executive agreements — to reduce the likelihood of the agreement being blocked in Congress.

Commander-in-chief

The president is entitled to send the USA's armed services into action. At the time that this power was conferred on the president, the USA had no standing army and the world's most powerful naval powers were over 3,000 miles (4,800 km) away in Europe, in an age when ships took several weeks to cross the Atlantic Ocean. Aircraft had not yet been invented. Moreover, with America's leaders being descendants of refugees from Europe, there was an expectation that the USA would avoid hostilities with the European powers. Today, in the age of supersonic travel, the USA's annual military budget roughly matches that of all other countries in the world combined.

Although the Founding Fathers had no concept of the USA as a global military superpower, they put in place a check on how the president could use his position as commander-in-chief. In an era when any prolonged military engagement was preceded by a formal declaration of war, the power to declare war was given to

Congress. Today, formal declarations are rare — even in the lengthy build-up to the conflict in Iraq in 2003 there was no suggestion that war would be declared.

This combination of immensely powerful armed forces, capable of being deployed anywhere in the world, and a largely redundant check on the president's use of those forces, has led to attempts to find new ways of imposing controls on the commander-in-chief:

- After the Vietnam War, which lasted over a decade and cost more than 50,000 American lives, Congress passed the War Powers Resolution in 1973. This forbids the president from authorising combat operations lasting longer than 60 days unless Congress has given its agreement or a declaration of war is made. However, the resolution has only been invoked twice, and on both occasions the president had already announced a withdrawal of forces, making the contribution of Congress merely cosmetic.
- In 2007, the Democrat-controlled Congress attached a timetable for the withdrawal of troops from Iraq to a bill providing funds for the war. The president simply announced that he would veto the bill unless the timetable was deleted and that the Democrats would be responsible for the death of any soldier killed as a result of a lack of funds. The Democrats yielded.

If Congress has proved an ineffective check on the commander-in-chief, a constraint has appeared in recent years from an unexpected source: the Supreme Court. Historically, the judiciary has avoided involvement in foreign and security matters, deferring to the executive. However, since President Bush, in his capacity of commander-in-chief, declared a 'war on terror' (in response to the attacks of 11 September 2001), which was followed by the arrest and detention without trial of people classified as 'enemy combatants', his policy has been challenged by the judiciary on three occasions:

- In *Rasul* v *Bush* (2004), the court ruled that detainees held on a US military base in Guantánamo Bay, Cuba, were entitled to the protection of the Constitution of the USA.
- In *Hamdan* v *Rumsfeld* (2006), the court ruled that the detainees could not be subject to military trials without the specific authorisation of Congress.
- The Republican majority in Congress responded to the *Hamdan* verdict by passing the Military Commissions Act. However, in *Boumediene* v *Bush* (2008), the court ruled that the Military Commissions Act was unconstitutional as it did not guarantee a fair trial.

Despite these challenges, by the time President Obama took office and ordered that plans be made for the dismantling of the detention centre at Guantánamo Bay, the executive had taken no active steps to comply with the court's rulings by either releasing or putting on trial the remaining detainees.

Head of state

As head of state, the president has a steady stream of ceremonial duties, none of which appears political in character. However, in this capacity he is effectively the symbol of his nation, and as long as he is seen this way he can use it to advance his political agenda. President Theodore Roosevelt referred to the opportunities to speak out on important issues to a national audience as the 'bully pulpit'. When allied to effective communication skills, the president can use his position as head of state to present himself as the father of the nation rather than a party politician. President F. D. Roosevelt (cousin to the president who coined the phrase 'bully pulpit') regularly gave radio broadcasts that sounded more like personal conversations than political speeches in order to persuade people of the benefits of his New Deal programme. President Reagan in the 1980s adopted a similar style to great effect.

This political asset can become a liability, however, if the president behaves in ways that are seen as inappropriate to a head of state. President Nixon, during the Watergate scandal, was seen as having damaged not just his personal reputation but those of the presidency and the nation. The same was true of President Clinton during the Monica Lewinsky scandal. And the record-low personal ratings of President Bush Jr when he left office can be traced to his use of his position as the symbol of the nation in the aftermath of 9/11, at a time of national unity, to promote his party and attack the opposition.

Party leader

As the person with the highest profile in his party, the president is effectively the leader of that party. He is expected to use his position to help raise funds for others running for office and to give his public support. This is especially important during the mid-term elections, when he has been in office for 2 years: if he is still popular, as President Bush Jr was in 2002, he can help his party win or retain control of Congress, which is an advantage when it comes to passing legislation.

However, as President Bush Jr discovered, it is difficult to balance the demands of head of state with those of party leader. His aggressive campaigning in 2002 turned him from a figure who united the country to one who divided it.

Overall assessment of the presidency

The president has limitations on all his powers except, perhaps, in his capacity as commander-in-chief. However, the nature of those constraints and their effectiveness varies according to his role. Moreover, the checks on his power do not always come from other branches: his position as head of government is sometimes made difficult by the people who are supposed to be working for him, and his position as head of state is only an asset if he has the good judgement and political skill to take advantage of being a national symbol.

Overall, there is something of a pattern to the effectiveness of the constraints imposed by other branches. Congress places considerable checks on the president in domestic matters. In foreign and security policy, however, congressional checks appear to have become increasingly ineffective over time. Indeed, in recent years, the main challenges to the president's security policy have come from the Supreme Court — which does not have the power to enforce its decisions.

Conclusion

To be in a position to tackle any questions on this topic, you need to have a strong understanding of:

- the roles of the president
- how the president carries out his roles
- the constraints on the president and their effectiveness
- the extent to which the president is the most powerful person in the world or is limited only to having the power to persuade

The ability to weigh up the strengths and weaknesses of the presidency is especially important for essays. You will *always* be expected to demonstrate different perspectives on issues, as this is how synoptic skills are tested.

Questions
&
Answers

This section looks at a range of answers to the kinds of questions you may face in your Unit 4C examination. It is divided into the four content areas identified in the specification: the Constitution, the Supreme Court, Congress and the presidency.

In the case of two of these topics (the Supreme Court and the presidency), the sample questions are short answers, worth 15 marks. In relation to the other two topics (the Constitution and Congress), the sample questions are essays, worth 45 marks. All questions are accompanied by two sample answers: one of A-grade standard and the other of C-grade standard. None of the answers is intended to be perfect. Each simply represents one way of approaching the question given.

Immediately after each answer you will find some guidance on how an examiner would approach allocating marks to it. This is indicated by the symbol 𝒆. An overall assessment of the strengths and weaknesses of each response is given. This is followed by an explanation of how the marks would be awarded according to the three assessment objectives (AOs).

The assessment objectives are:
- **AO1** Demonstrate knowledge and understanding of relevant institutions, processes, political concepts, theories and debates.
- **AO2** Analyse and evaluate political information, arguments and explanations, and identify parallels, connections, similarities and differences between aspects of the political systems studied.
- **AO3** Construct and communicate coherent arguments, making use of a range of appropriate political vocabulary.

Marks for short-answer questions are allocated as follows:
AO1 = 5 marks
AO2 = 7 marks
AO3 = 3 marks
Total = 15 marks

Marks for essay questions are allocated as follows:
AO1 = 12 marks
AO2 = 24 marks (includes 12 marks for synopticity)
AO3 = 9 marks
Total = 45 marks

Ideally, you should attempt the questions provided here before you read the answers given. Once you have done this, you can review your work in light of the examiner's advice and comments. Remember, these answers are *not* model answers for you to learn and reproduce in the examination. It is unlikely that the questions in the examination will be worded exactly as they are here and, in any case, there is always more than one way of addressing any question.

The Constitution

Discuss the effectiveness of constitutional protection of freedom. (45 marks)

■ ■ ■

A-grade answer

The US Constitution was designed to ensure that politicians could never become powerful enough to deny freedom to Americans. However, Americans disagree on the extent to which this goal has been achieved.

There is, of course, no disagreement about how the Constitution *ought* to protect freedom. The Founding Fathers intended to make sure that freedoms could not be infringed by powerful individuals or groups by making it impossible to acquire excessive power. To ensure this outcome, they created a political system in which there would be strict separation of power. No one can be in more than one branch of the federal government at the same time. They also created a system of checks and balances, with a special emphasis on ensuring that the executive branch would face severe constraints on its power, as they saw this as the most dangerous branch of government that could easily become a tyranny if the checks were not effective. Also, to protect against a group of people working together across the different branches of government to build their power, each group within the federal government comes to office in different ways and at different times. The president is chosen by the whole country through an Electoral College, the Senators were originally chosen by their state legislators, members of the House of Representatives are chosen by the people of a local area and Supreme Court judges are appointed. In addition, the Bill of Rights was intended to ensure that even if politicians worked together and had popular support to infringe the rights of (say) a minority group, they would not find it easy to do so.

With freedom protected in so many ways, it may come as a surprise that not all Americans believe that the Constitution has worked well. However, this is not so much the fault of the Constitution but the different ways in which 'freedom' is defined.

For those on the left of the political spectrum, 'freedom' means the ability of people to make the most of their potential. Sometimes, a strong government is needed in order to provide people with the best circumstances to make the most of their potential. This may mean providing schools and libraries for people to develop their intellect, or it may mean providing facilities for people to develop their sporting potential. However, the political system makes it difficult for the government to play this kind of role when it wishes to. Even something as fundamental as schools is not the responsibility of the national government because of federalism, and every attempt to set up a national health service has, so far, failed.

question

In addition to being severely limited in providing support for people, left-wingers in America are often frustrated by their limitations in providing protection for people. The greatest obstacle to people and groups developing their potential, apart from a lack of facilities, is discrimination because they are denied opportunities. Discrimination has been a problem in the USA since the country was founded. Black Americans were enslaved, women did not get the vote until the twentieth century and there is still an issue of equal rights for gay people. Although there has been progress for all these people, almost certainly there would have been more rapid progress if the Constitution had not protected prejudiced people in positions of power at local level from government intervention.

However, left-wingers do give the political system credit for being flexible enough to enable the government to respond to a massive crisis. In the 1930s, the Supreme Court at first resisted the introduction of the New Deal programmes that were intended to help those who could no longer help themselves, on the grounds that they undermined the system of federalism. However, they came to realise that the programmes were essential and accepted that the balance of power between the federal government and the states had to change.

Although people on the left criticise the system of federalism for hindering government efforts to help people, on the right the greatest concern is that the system of federalism has not been strong enough. This concern comes from the view that 'freedom' means not being interfered with by the government. People on the right would prefer that even local politicians, who understand the needs of local citizens, interfere as little as possible, and they see the growth of the federal government as bordering on tyranny. As the hero of the right, Ronald Reagan, put it, 'the nine most dangerous words in the English language are "I'm from the government and I'm here to help"'.

For people on the right, therefore, the fact that the federal government has grown in size and scope to such an extent since the Constitution was written is proof that freedom has not been protected. What was once three departments with a few hundred employees has become 15 departments with around 2 million employees. And, each time there is a new national crisis, the government gets bigger. There was the New Deal, then the Second World War and, more recently, the attacks of 9/11 that led to the setting up of the Department of Homeland Security and the economic slump that has resulted in the government borrowing trillions of dollars and dictating to state government how it should be spent.

However, just as people on the left praise as well as criticise the Constitution, people on the right see the failure of the Great Society programme as evidence that the Constitution at least places some limits on the scope of the federal government. As the Great Society was not a response to a crisis but a political choice to expand government intervention to eradicate poverty, conservatives are reassured that the American people will only accept government growth if they think it is essential.

Also, conservatives believe that it is possible to strengthen the existing constitutional protections against a larger federal government by passing a constitutional amendment for a balanced budget. In the 1980s, this goal was almost achieved.

For people who fall between the two extremes of right and left, the focus is less on the faults of the Constitution and more on its strengths. People in the centre of the political spectrum acknowledge some faults in the way the Constitution works in practice, mainly that it is more effective at correcting infringements in freedom than it is at preventing them. For example, the Constitution did not prevent the loss of liberty of African-Americans during slavery and segregation and it also did not prevent the loss of liberty of Japanese Americans who were interned in camps during the Second World War. However, these issues were eventually resolved.

It could be argued that America is going through a similar process at the moment. After 9/11, the government established a camp at Guantánamo Bay that seemed to many to be in violation of both international law and the US Constitution. When civil rights groups appealed to the Supreme Court to declare the government's actions to be unconstitutional the court ruled in their favour each time, even though the courts traditionally do not get involved in national security matters. This demonstrates that the culture of freedom that springs from the Constitution, and resistance to governmental efforts to limit freedom, are so strong that a minimum level of freedom will always be protected in the end.

Overall, therefore, how effective the Constitution is at protecting freedom depends mainly on people's point of view, but almost all Americans agree that it is good at protecting freedom to some extent.

e This response gets off to a slow start, appearing to describe rather than evaluate the constitutional protections of freedom. However, after the second paragraph it develops the idea that the key issue being discussed is contrasting concepts of freedom. This approach enables the candidate to demonstrate a strong understanding of the Constitution.

Most of the essay covers the contrasting views on the effectiveness of the constitutional protection of freedom, with each ideological perspective outlined and illustrated. Each viewpoint is explained well, although there is clearly scope for greater depth and sophistication.

Overall, therefore, the response achieves the top grade but not the very top marks.

Marks
AO1 = 9
AO2 = 9 + 10 (for synopticity)
AO3 = 7
Total = 35 marks

question

C-grade answer

The Constitution of the USA aims to protect freedom in a variety of ways, but some of them are more effective than others.

There is a system of separation of powers in America that is designed to protect ordinary people from politicians becoming too powerful. Each branch of government has its own specific responsibilities and the system of separation of powers should make sure that none of them expands its powers beyond the limits that the Constitution places on it.

In practice, this system has not worked out in the way that the Founding Fathers had in mind. The legislature was supposed to be the most important branch, which is why it is the subject of Article 1 of the Constitution. However, most people would agree that the executive branch is more significant, which the Founding Fathers wanted to avoid. And the Supreme Court, with the power of judicial review (which was not in the Constitution), is far more powerful than was originally intended. Despite this, none of the branches has become tyrannical. The president is able to do more than the Founding Fathers wanted but he is not able to do anything he likes. He does face a lot of checks from the other two branches, such as Congress confirming all his appointments and the Supreme Court overruling actions of the president that exceed his powers.

As well as separation of powers, the Constitution limits the ability of politicians working together to increase their powers by staggering elections. There is never a time when all the people who hold positions of power in Washington DC are elected at the same time. Members of the House of Representatives are elected every 2 years. The president is elected every 4 years, and because of the Twenty-Second Amendment he can only serve two terms. The Senators face re-election every 6 years. This means that even if a situation arises in which one party wins a majority in both houses of Congress and the presidency at the same time, it will not hold all that power for long if it misuses it. The members of the House of Representatives would have to be aware that within 2 years they will be held to account by the public. Also, the different timescales means that politicians will usually have different priorities, with the House of Representatives needing to achieve things within 2 years while the Senate has 6 years to achieve things. This also makes it less likely that politicians in different institutions will cooperate with each other to expand their powers, even if they are in the same party.

The Constitution also contains the Bill of Rights. This is the first ten amendments to the Constitution and they had to be adopted for some of the original 13 states to ratify the Constitution as they were concerned that the other protections of freedom would be inadequate. The Bill of Rights is designed to make sure that even if one of the branches of government became too powerful or people in different branches worked together to increase their powers, there would be some rights that they would not be able to touch. It covers the most important freedoms such as free speech, the right to demonstrate, freedom of religion and, most importantly, the right of habeas corpus that makes it unconstitutional for the government to make people 'disappear' in ways that are seen in modern tyrannies such as Burma. The Bill of Rights has proved an effective protection of freedom, as the Supreme Court has been able to use it to update what rights mean in today's world, such as the right to an abortion, and put limits on the ability of the government to infringe those rights. However, some aspects of the Bill of Rights have become obsolete, such as the Third Amendment that protects homeowners from having to provide shelter for soldiers.

The final constitutional protection of freedom is federalism. This was intended to make sure that the national government could never become as powerful as the central government in Britain that it had broken away from. It gives sovereignty over some matters to the national government and sovereignty over other matters to the states. Originally, in an arrangement known as 'dual federalism', the national government only had responsibility for foreign affairs and interstate disputes, with all other matters 'reserved' to the states. However, this has changed over time. The central government grew during the Great Depression of the 1930s when the 'New Deal' was introduced, leading to 'cooperative federalism', and it grew again in the 1960s during President Johnson's 'Great Society' programme that led to 'creative federalism'. All this shows that federalism has not been an effective way of protecting people from the national government becoming too powerful. In addition, attempts to turn the clock back to dual federalism, through 'new federalism', have clearly not worked. However, there have been times when the states have not been able to do enough for their citizens, such as during the Great Depression, and it has been an advantage that the national government has been able to step in and solve the crisis.

Overall, the constitutional protections of freedom have had a mixed record, with some, especially the Bill of Rights, being much more effective than others. Most importantly, however, America has never suffered the kind of tyranny that the Founding Fathers feared, even when the system has not worked in the ways that they intended.

This is a knowledgeable account of the ways in which the Constitution is designed to protect freedom and there are assessments of how well each of them works. However, the approach adopted tends to be descriptive rather than analytical and, because the account does not clearly provide contrasting viewpoints, it is not synoptic in character.

The question asks for a discussion of a topic area but it does not give a clear indication of the direction that the discussion should take. When responding to this style of question, you should begin by setting out the area of debate that you will

question

explore. This increases the likelihood that you will discuss the different viewpoints in your chosen area of debate, which is an important feature of A2 politics essays.

Marks
AO1 = 9
AO2 = 5 + 3 (for synopticity)
AO3 = 4
Total = 21 marks

The Supreme Court

Why has judicial activism been controversial? (15 marks)

■ ■ ■

A-grade answer

The way in which judges make use of the power of judicial review has been controversial since the Supreme Court decided that interpreting the Constitution was the responsibility of the federal judiciary in the case of *Marbury* v *Madison* in 1803.

The ability to interpret the Constitution gives the judiciary tremendous power. Every law in the land, plus every governmental action, is in principle governed by the Constitution. This means that these laws and actions are governed by the Supreme Court's interpretation of what the Constitution means. This makes the nine judges on the court the most powerful group of people in the country. Yet they are not subject to election and therefore cannot be held accountable for their decisions.

For some people in the USA, so much power in the hands of a small number of people is highly undesirable. They believe that the Founding Fathers, when they created the Constitution, intended to prevent any group of people from holding so much power, as it was seen as a recipe for tyranny. As a result, even though it is not possible to take the power of judicial review away from the judges, it is important that they use their powers with great caution. People who hold this view (judicial restraint) argue that judges are constantly in danger of destroying the system of checks and balances by exercising far more power than Congress or the president through judgements that overrule them and that there are no effective checks on the judiciary when they do this. As a result, if judges are to be faithful to the spirit of the Constitution, they should only use their powers when absolutely necessary. The rest of the time they should leave policy decisions to the elected branches of government, who can scrutinise each other's decisions or actions and be held to account by the voters.

Other Americans see the situation completely differently. They believe that while the Founding Fathers were concerned about tyranny coming from the concentration of power, the creators of the Constitution were also concerned about tyranny of the majority. Some of the most important aspects of the Constitution were designed to protect people from the majority, and their elected representatives, because they might be willing to take rights away from minority groups they do not like. For example, during the era of segregation, the white majority in the South denied rights to African-Americans through the democratic process. Under circumstances such as these, it is the responsibility of judges, who do not have to worry about popularity, as they are not elected, to ensure that constitutional rights are upheld, even if this is not what the majority want. They did this in 1954, in the case of *Brown* v *Board of Education*. The importance of protecting rights is the reason that people who hold this view support judicial activism.

The debate between judicial restraint and judicial activism is also highly controversial because it overlaps with other bitter political disputes. Supporters of judicial restraint tend to be conservatives who do not favour radical change, especially when it benefits minorities. Their objections grow even more forceful when political reforms that favour minorities are made by the courts and the democratic majority is unable to overturn them. So, they strongly criticised the ruling of *Lawrence* v *Texas* in 2003 that extended gay rights and seemed to open the door to gay marriage in the future. On the other hand, supporters of judicial activism tend to be liberals who believe that, as social attitudes change, the way that the Constitution is understood should also change. For that reason they applauded the *Lawrence* v *Texas* decision. If gay rights had to wait until there was a clear majority across the country in support of changing the law, it would have to wait for many years, possibly even generations. Judicial activism makes such delays unnecessary.

 This response demonstrates a strong grasp of the most challenging aspect of this question, that both supporters and opponents of judicial activism justify their position by claiming that their views are faithful to the core principles of the Constitution. Opponents of judicial activism focus on the concentration of power and the lack of accountability. Supporters of judicial activism focus on the dangers of the tyranny of the majority and the importance of protecting rights.

The response then goes one step further by recognising that the debate on judicial philosophies is part of a wider ideological debate on the most appropriate policies for the country.

The most obvious weakness of the response is the comparative lack of cases used to illustrate the points being made. The fact that the candidate is able to cite accurately (with dates) the cases of *Marbury* v *Madison* and *Lawrence* v *Texas*, as well as the widely used case of *Brown* v *Board of Education*, suggests that more examples could be used. Examiners will only give credit for the knowledge demonstrated.

Marks
AO1 = 3
AO2 = 6
AO3 = 3
Total = 12 marks

■ ■ ■

C-grade answer

Judicial activism is controversial because it leads to unelected judges taking ever greater powers for themselves, which undermines democracy and the Constitution.

The Constitution did not give the Supreme Court the power of judicial review. The court gave itself this power in the case of *Marbury* v *Madison*. It is open to question whether this was ever valid. The Constitution clearly gave policy-making responsibilities only to those who could be held to account by the American people, and the most important powers, such as raising and spending taxes, were given to those who would be held to account frequently — every 2 years. The power of judicial review is greater than the powers given to either of the elected branches of the federal government, yet it is wielded by people who are not answerable to anyone.

This has become an ever-increasing problem since left-wingers gained control of the court in the 1950s. Whether or not everyone agrees with it, the system of racial groups living largely separate lives was the will of the majority of the population in the southern states and a part of the culture of that region of the country. The Founding Fathers clearly intended that the system of federalism would allow regional variations such as this and anyone who did not like the southern way of life was free to leave — and many did. When the court overturned the laws supported by the majority in the South in *Brown* v *Board of Education*, they not only weakened the democratic system but also the principle of federalism that is the most important protection against an oppressive federal government.

As the respected jurist Robert Bork says, when judges interpret the Constitution they read into it their own views. This is illustrated by the case of *Roe* v *Wade*. The Supreme Court justified its decision to declare abortion a constitutional right on the grounds that the Constitution contains a right to privacy and that it is a woman's right to make a private decision as to whether or not she should terminate her pregnancy. No one seriously questions that the Constitution protects unspecified rights under the Ninth Amendment, but in this case the court could have just as easily ruled that there is a right to life for the unborn baby. Concluding that there is a constitutional right to privacy, therefore, is nothing more than the personal views of the judges on the court at the time — arbitrary political decision-making associated with medieval kings that the Founding Fathers intended to prevent.

Even the appointment of conservative judges by a series of Republican presidents since the early 1970s has done little to protect the American people from judicial activism. In the recent case of *Kennedy* v *Louisiana*, the court ruled that it was unconstitutional to impose the death penalty on child rapists on the grounds that there was a national consensus against such a severe punishment for the crime. But the conservative minority on the court pointed out that the evidence could be interpreted to support the *opposite* conclusion. Even Barack Obama criticised the court's reasoning.

In the end, in each of these cases, it is not the Constitution that is the basis for far-reaching judgements but the personal views of the judges, hence the controversial nature of judicial activism.

question

Students often ask whether they are allowed to express their own views in responses to exam questions. The answer is that the examiner is mainly concerned with a candidate's ability to weigh up both sides of an issue. If the candidate's strongly held personal views help achieve this outcome, then they are an asset. If, however, the candidate's views make it difficult to take a balanced approach to the issue, then they become a liability. In the case of this response, the candidate demonstrates such a strong grasp of one side of the issue that it is hard to believe that he or she does not have an understanding of the other side. However, because it is a well-informed attack on judicial activism from a conservative perspective, the answer is unbalanced. An examiner may reasonably infer that the candidate has the knowledge and academic ability to provide a more complete response, but marks can only be given for what is actually produced, not for what could potentially be produced.

Marks
AO1 = 3
AO2 = 4
AO3 = 2
Total = 9 marks

Congress

'Members of Congress serve their constituents well but their nation badly.' Discuss.

(45 marks)

A-grade answer

Members of Congress have a reputation for putting the interests of their constituents ahead of all other political factors such as their party or even the nation. However, this essay will argue that this is a reputation that is not deserved and, therefore, that the quotation is inaccurate. Rather, when members of Congress are making political choices, they take a range of factors into account.

Congress is responsible for overseeing the executive departments. In this capacity, its members monitor the ways in which the departments implement federal law. Each member of Congress, in both the House of Representatives and the Senate, is a member of at least one committee. Because of the strict separation of powers, members of Congress build their political careers in the legislature, and this is usually done through building expertise in the issues covered by their committee. This expertise, together with the extensive support provided by specialist staff, is used to monitor closely the work of the government department scrutinised by their committee. While they will pay close attention to the way in which particular policies affect their constituents, most of the work of the committees has a far broader focus. In fact, the main criticism faced by congressional committees is that they are too willing to build links with pressure groups, which leads to the formation of iron triangles.

Members of Congress can also be defended from the accusation that they put their constituents first when their role as investigators is considered. When Hurricane Katrina struck New Orleans in 2005, killing many residents, concern about the causes and consequences went far further than the members of Congress from Louisiana and neighbouring states. Nine congressional committees investigated the events and produced reports. Also, when Congress investigated President Clinton during the Monica Lewinsky affair, it was mainly party considerations that proved most significant, with the Republicans attacking the president and the Democrats defending him.

The appointments process, which usually has little direct impact on constituents, is taken seriously by the Senate. All nominees put forward by the president are carefully scrutinised by the Senators. If they think that someone is unqualified for the position, such as when Harriet Miers was put forward for the Supreme Court, they are willing to make it clear that they will not go ahead with the confirmation. In this case, this occurred even though the majority in the Senate was from the same party as the president. The same happened to one of President Obama's appointees. It was revealed that his nominee for Health Secretary, Tom Daschle, had not paid taxes on a limousine and driver provided by a health-services company. These close links with the industry he would be in charge of forced his withdrawal.

Congress closely examines all legislation presented to it. Unlike in parliamentary democracies, where the government and legislature are from the same party, all bills are significantly amended in the USA, and a high proportion of them are completely rejected. This is what the Founding Fathers had in mind when they drew up a constitution based on strict separation of powers and checks and balances, and indicates that Congress fulfils its constitutional role of ensuring that the executive branch cannot make decisions without the agreement of the representatives of the people.

Even in foreign affairs, where Congress is often seen as not very effective, it can be argued that Congress does its best to serve the nation well. All treaties negotiated by the president have to be ratified by the Senate by a two-thirds majority. On a few occasions the Senate has rejected treaties. More significantly, however, presidents have avoided signing treaties so that they will not have to submit them for ratification. Instead, they have preferred to sign executive agreements. The fact that presidents feel the need to avoid having to submit treaties to the Senate shows that they take this check on their foreign policy powers seriously.

Why then is it suggested that members of Congress always put their constituents first? Principally this is because the frequency of elections puts pressure on Congressmen to make sure that they have been seen to take care of their constituents on a regular basis. Members of the House of Representatives have elections every 2 years. They know that any challengers will criticise them as ineffective if they cannot demonstrate that they have brought benefits to their districts. For this reason, members of Congress engage in 'pork-barrel' politics. This means that they vote for any bill that adds jobs or resources to their districts. And if a bill does not have this effect, they make amendments to bills, called 'earmarks', that result in federal funds being spent in their district.

Some people argue that this leads to vast sums of money being wasted on projects that will help the popularity of the members of Congress but are not good for the country. In recent years, the 'bridge to nowhere' in Alaska has been used as an example of how Congress wastes money, as the proposed bridge was to link two small communities at massive cost.

It is also argued that members of Congress are reluctant to raise taxes, which are always unpopular, to pay for these expensive projects. This means that the country almost always operates at a deficit. Over the past four decades there has only been a short period when the country ran a budget surplus: in the final years of the presidency of Bill Clinton.

However, the pressure arising from frequent elections only applies to the House of Representatives. As a result, the Senate often provides a moderating influence on spending. Thus, in early 2009, when the president's stimulus package was going through Congress, the Senate helped to drive down its cost from the original $825 billion to $790 billion because of concerns of the impact of the deficit on future generations.

Also, it has to be recognised that the majority of 'pork-barrel' projects bring much needed jobs and practical improvements to the districts that benefit from them, for example improved roads and public transport. Thus much of the so-called 'pork' is valuable and even essential. The collapse of a road bridge in Minneapolis in 2007 was blamed by some on inadequate spending. What is more, some of the most obviously wasteful projects do not go ahead because of public and media pressure. The famous 'bridge to nowhere' was eventually scrapped, and the Alaska Senator who claimed credit for including it in legislation lost his seat in the next election.

Overall, therefore, while there is a widespread perception that Congress is guilty of localism and waste, close analysis does not justify this view. Clearly, 'pork-barrel' politics can justifiably be criticised but there is a great deal more to the work of Congress than attaching earmarks to bills.

This response adopts a traditional approach to writing an essay that seeks to make an effective argument. It begins by taking a clear stance on the question: it firmly establishes that it will attempt to support a conclusion that the quotation in the title, criticising the work of Congress, cannot be justified.

It then goes on to outline the arguments that support this conclusion, with the theme being that Congress has a variety of roles, most of which do not necessarily have any great significance for the members' constituents and which cannot be conducted properly if the members adopt a narrow, local approach. In developing this theme, the essay is both describing how Congress operates and analysing why much of the work of Congress is to be admired.

The third part of the essay examines why Congress is criticised. This leads to the development of a counter-argument that is essential to demonstrating synoptic skills — the ability to discuss at least two viewpoints — for which the examiner also awards marks.

The essay then sets out the weaknesses in the arguments criticising Congress. In the conclusion it explains why the first set of arguments outweighs the second set, thereby demonstrating the ability to evaluate viewpoints — for which the examiner also awards marks.

Overall, this approach leads to the construction of a coherent argument, a fourth skill for which the examiner awards marks.

It is this steady accumulation of marks for different skills, in a piece of written work that seamlessly develops a theme, that makes this an A-grade response. Moreover, had the response taken this approach to reach the opposite conclusion, it would receive the same grade, provided it sustained the argument as effectively. Examiners

question

are not concerned with which conclusion candidates reach, only how well they support that conclusion.

This is not to say that this essay is perfect. When acknowledging that there may be legitimate criticisms of Congress, a limited number of points are made (e.g. pork-barrel politics which, combined with a reluctance to raise taxes, leads to deficit spending). Also, there is no acknowledgement that this is a powerful argument. However, an essay does not have to be perfect to achieve the highest grade.

Marks

AO1 = 10
AO2 = 10 + 10 (for synopticity)
AO3 = 8
Total = 38 marks

■ ■ ■

C-grade answer

On one hand it could be argued that the members of Congress pay attention to their constituents at the expense of more important issues. On the other hand, it can be argued that when Congress is dealing with issues that their constituents are not very interested in, they are quite good at serving the national interest. This essay will consider both points of view.

The complaint that members of Congress always put their constituents first is linked to the view that the highest priority of Congressmen is to get re-elected and that this means that their voters have to be their highest priority. As a result, members of Congress aim to ensure that they have some concrete achievements to show the electorate before the next election. This means securing as many benefits for their districts as possible, a political strategy known as pork-barrel politics.

As all members of Congress face the same pressures, regardless of party, they have an incentive to engage in pork-barrel politics and to help each other. In a process called log-rolling, they cooperate with each other by exchanging votes. If a member of Congress in one region of the country will not be affected by a proposal that will benefit voters in another area (for example snow ploughs in Alaska), he or she will vote for it in exchange for support for a proposal with similar effects (for example subsidies for orange-juice production in Florida).

The problem with pork-barrel politics and log-rolling is that they lead to a steady increase in government expenditure, which may not benefit the national economy. Hence the claim that members of Congress do not serve the national interest well. However, they virtually guarantee re-election and provide practical benefits for ordinary Americans, so they are good for both politicians and voters. Hence the claim that members serve their constituents well.

Members of Congress also go to great lengths to make themselves accessible to their constituents. They all have websites and a large staff who can handle phone calls, letters and e-mails. They have staff who can deal with inquiries in Washington DC and in their districts. And whenever Congress is not in session, they make a point of ensuring that they are seen around their districts and attending events where they will meet their constituents in person. Compared to representatives in other countries, they do not present themselves as too important to make time for ordinary people.

However, there is more to the work of Congress than providing resources for their districts and states. Congress has to legislate in the best interests of the country. This means carefully scrutinising all bills, especially those proposed by the president, and making amendments to improve them. Some of these amendments take the form of earmarks for the benefit of their constituents, but most of them have little or nothing to do with pork barrel politics. Indeed, it has been claimed that no more than 2% of the federal budget can be described as earmarks. Most of their scrutiny of legislation, therefore, relates to the impact it will have on national life, and if members of Congress believe that it is not in the best interests of the country they will not hesitate to amend or reject it. This process also benefits from the tendency of members of Congress to get regularly re-elected. Over time, they develop great expertise that is applied to the process of scrutinising legislation.

Congress is also responsible for scrutinising the work of the executive branch of government. Much of this work is quite dull and unglamorous, examining thousands of pages of regulations or asking witnesses about technical regulations. Yet it is extremely important as Congress has a constitutional responsibility to monitor how the executive branch is using its powers. Most constituents have little interest in this work. However, both the public and the press are extremely critical of Congress if it is shown that the executive has not been doing its job properly and that Congress has failed to intervene. This was demonstrated by Hurricane Katrina. The federal government was responsible for the flood defences around New Orleans and was aware that they could not withstand a Category 5 hurricane, yet made no effort to strengthen them and had no effective emergency evacuation procedures. Congress did not recognise these failings until too late. As a result, it was not only the executive branch that was criticised for the deaths of New Orleans residents following the hurricane but also Congress.

On balance, therefore, while there is a case for claiming that members of Congress are always very aware that they need to convince their constituents that they are looking after their interests while in Washington DC, members of Congress do not neglect their responsibilities to the nation as a whole.

📝 This candidate has as much material at his or her disposal as the A-grade candidate but uses it far less effectively. Both recognise that members of Congress have several roles and that the question they are answering implies that they put their representative role before all others. However, this response is limited to examining each role in turn, leading to the conclusion that constituents are not necessarily put first when legislation is being considered by Congress or when it is scrutinising the executive.

Towards the end, the argument loses its way. It is not clear whether the candidate is arguing that Congress plays an important scrutiny role or whether Congress is being criticised for not playing that role effectively.

A further criticism is that the answer lacks illustrations, except for general examples (that Alaska and Florida have, broadly, different interests) and Hurricane Katrina.

Overall, therefore, while the candidate displays understanding of the roles of Congress and demonstrates some synoptic skills by recognising that there are a range of ways of looking at the work of Congress, the argument lacks depth and provides only one illustration to support points that it is making. The result is that this reasonably well-informed candidate has produced a response that may just reach a Grade C and could legitimately be awarded a Grade D.

Marks
AO1 = 9
AO2 = 6 + 3 (for synopticity)
AO3 = 4
Total = 22 marks

uestion

The presidency

Assess how much control the president has over the executive branch.   (15 marks)

■ ■ ■

A-grade answer

Although the president is often described as the 'most powerful person in the world', he faces considerable constraints in his role as head of government.

When forming his government he wants to choose the best people possible to head the government departments. However, the president has to consider a range of factors in addition to the abilities of the candidates. First, he has to persuade people to leave their existing posts, move to Washington DC and, in many cases, accept a pay cut. Not surprisingly, many excellent candidates at the top of their professions decline job offers from the president. Also, there is an expectation that the president's cabinet will 'look like America'. This means appointing a racially diverse cabinet, with women and all regions of the country represented at the highest levels of government. President Obama's most senior cabinet members when he first took office included a woman (Hillary Clinton), an African-American (Eric Holder) and a Republican (Robert Gates). In addition, the president's choices have to be confirmed by the Senate. Controversial figures, such as President George H. W. Bush's nominee for defense secretary, John Tower, may be rejected. More often, the intense scrutiny that comes with the Senate confirmation process can lead to candidates withdrawing, such as Tom Daschle, who was President Obama's choice as health secretary but who pulled out of the process because of revelations that he had not paid all his taxes.

Once his government is in place, the president may have difficulty in getting it to implement his policies. His cabinet, drawn from so many different places, often does not act as team but as individual heads of department with different agendas. Under almost all presidents, the defense secretary and secretary of state have a difficult working relationship — even Donald Rumsfeld and Colin Powell, who were close colleagues in the administration of President Bush Snr. As a consequence, the president often has difficulty in getting the whole government to produce 'joined-up' policies.

Civil servants also pose a challenge to presidential control over the executive branch. The federal bureaucracy likes to think of itself as relatively independent. It generally has long-term aims that may not correspond with the president's short-term goals. These factors may make it difficult to make civil servants implement policies that reverse those that they have been working on for a long time. Also, government departments are answerable to Congress as well as the president, as it is Congress that sets their budget and has oversight over the departments' work.

questions & answers

This can be used as a justification for failing to wholeheartedly implement the president's plans.

However, despite all these obstacles, the president does have a variety of ways of exerting control over the government departments. As well as appointing the heads of departments, who ought to be loyal to the president, he can also appoint people to be his 'eyes and ears' to work alongside the civil servants. This is known as the 'spoils system', and the president is entitled to appoint people to work alongside the senior policy makers, the managers of the different sections in the departments (these are known as schedule C appointments) and the civil servants who actually implement the policies. Also, the president has the Executive Office of the Presidency (EOP) that exists to help him implement his agenda. The EOP can monitor the work of different departments and put pressure on the leaders of any department that appears not to be developing the president's agenda. It also plays an important role in coordination across departments. For example, the national security advisor serves to ensure that the State Department, the Defense Department and the security services are all working together on key foreign-policy issues and not working against each other as they tend to do in cabinet.

Overall, therefore, while the president may have great difficulty controlling the executive branch, he does have some instruments that ensure that it does not simply ignore his political priorities.

This response demonstrates many of the features found in excellent short-answer questions. While short answers often do not need an introductory paragraph, in this case it is sensible to begin with a brief clarification of the question, identifying that it is about the president's role as head of government (referred to as 'chief executive' in some textbooks).

The answer then goes on to identify the main challenges that the president faces and how he may address these. This is a good structure for a short answer.

In outlining the challenges faced by the president, this response logically explains first the difficulties faced in forming a government and then the difficulties of managing the government once it has been formed. There are some additional challenges that are not mentioned, such as the tendency for heads of department to 'go native' and adopt the department's priorities rather than those of the president, the impact of pressure groups working with civil servants and congressional committees (iron triangles) to thwart the will of the president, and the fact that some federal agencies and commissions are largely independent of presidential control, such as the Federal Reserve. However, examiners do not expect every possible issue to be covered in the 15 minutes available to answer a short-answer question, so these oversights would make little difference to the final mark. The most important issue here is that three substantial points are made, explained well and illustrated with a range of relevant examples.

Furthermore, the response considers the other side of the question by examining the ways in which the president is able to influence the departments, again providing a good explanation and an illustration.

Overall, this response provides almost everything in terms of knowledge, analysis and structure that an examiner would want from a short-answer question.

Marks
AO1 = 4
AO2 = 6
AO3 = 3
Total = 13 marks

C-grade answer

The president has only limited control over the executive branch because of the relatively limited control he has over his cabinet. However, this is compensated for, to some extent, by the support he gets from the Executive Office of the Presidency.

Presidents often do not find the cabinet useful to them for several reasons. The first is that a president cannot always appoint his first choice, as all regions of the country should be represented in the cabinet. For example, the secretary of the interior has traditionally been someone from a western state with experience of land policy and conservation issues, while the secretary of labor is traditionally someone who is acceptable to trade unions. This raises the second point, that pressure groups have to be considered when appointments are made. Third, all sections of the population should be represented, including women and ethnic minorities. Fourth, the number and responsibilities of cabinet secretaries cannot be changed except by Act of Congress, which means that, compared to the prime minister of the UK, the president has little flexibility when it comes to organising the government in ways that are compatible with his political priorities. Finally, the president's nominees all have to be confirmed by the Senate and this may result in some of them not being appointed.

On the other hand, the president does have the Executive Office of the Presidency to help him achieve his goals. This was set up in the 1930s when the Brownlow Committee reported that the 'president needs help'. The Executive Office has been a great source of support to presidents as governing has become more complex. He is able to appoint people whom he personally knows and trusts (unlike members of the cabinet) and who can be relied on to be completely loyal to him. They do not need to be confirmed by the Senate, so there is no risk of him having to turn to people who are not his first choice. They help him coordinate the work of the government departments and put pressure on any cabinet secretary who appears to have greater loyalty to his or her department than to the president. The president is particularly dependent on the Executive Office of the Presidency when there are important decisions to be made at times of crisis and he wants to be sure that the advice he is getting is coming from people that he can rely on.

In addition, while presidents often find that the cabinet as a whole is not useful to them, individual members can be valuable when policy is being made, especially 'top-tier' members such as the secretary of defense.

On balance, therefore, while the president has only limited control over the executive branch through the cabinet, he has more control through the Executive Office of the Presidency.

This response demonstrates that the candidate has some knowledge of how the executive branch of government operates and provides some analysis of the strengths and weaknesses of presidents in exerting control. However, it would only be awarded a C grade, probably at the C/D boundary.

This is because the candidate is attempting to provide an adapted version of a pre-prepared response to the question. In the past, exams have asked about the relative significance of the cabinet and the Executive Office of the Presidency. This candidate has clearly prepared for the possibility of the question appearing again and, seeing a question that is similar, has provided the pre-learned series of points from the earlier mark scheme. The result is a list, with little development and no recent illustrations, that has some relevance to the question but fails to provide a detailed and complete response. It is particularly noteworthy that not a single example is provided, suggesting that the candidate has not make much use of his or her textbook or followed current affairs closely throughout the course.

You should be aware that, at the start of the marking process, examiners are warned to look out for this type of answer. Such answers do little to demonstrate any great depth of understanding and are rewarded accordingly.

Overall, this response demonstrates the dangers of relying too heavily on model answers.

Marks
AO1 = 3
AO2 = 3
AO3 = 2
Total = 8 marks